The Tale of Two Bridges

adapted by
Barbara Maddox

**Based on the diary of Colonel
R.G. Pine-Coffin, DSO., MC.,
The 7th (Light Infantry) Parachute Battalion**

© Barbara Maddox and Peter Pine-Coffin 2003

The Tale of Two Bridges

Published by Peter Pine-Coffin,
Walters Cottage, Graffham, Petworth West Sussex, GU28 0NP.

The right of Peter Pine-Coffin is to be identified as
the publisher of this book, which has been asserted by
Peter Pine-Coffin in accordance with the
Copyright, Designs and Patents Act 1988.

All rights are reserved.

This book nor any part of the contents may be
reproduced or transmitted by any means, electronic or mechanical.
No recording or photocopying, storing or retrieval in any form
is permitted without the written consent of the publisher.

Printed and distributed by
KerryType Ltd., Midhurst, West Sussex, GU29 9PX.

The first edition was limited to 1,000 numbered copies.
First published in Great Britain, November 2003.

Second revised edition.
Published in Great Britain, May 2004.

Front cover photographs courtesy Airborne Forces Museum

Contents

Foreword by H.R.H. The Prince of Wales	iv
Dedication	vii
Author's Acknowledgements	viii
Acknowledgements	ix
Prologue	x
Every Man An Emperor	xii
War Declared	xiii
Appointments - Normandy	xiv
Order of Battle	xvi
Chapter 1 - Go To It	1
Chapter 2 - The Task	14
Chapter 3 - Floating Down Over France	24
Poem	31
Chapter 4 - Action	32
Chapter 5 - The Battle Continues	44
Chapter 6 - The Divisional Bridgehead	58
Chapter 7 - Bob's Farm	74
Chapter 8 - The Break Out	94
Chapter 9 - More Anecdotes	116
Grangues Memorial	141
Song Sheet	170
Letter of Freedom of the Town of Bénouville	172
Normandy Pilgrimage 1955	173
Some acronyms used in this book	174
Index	176
7th Para Memorial	180
Prayer of Airborne Forces	184

Foreword
by
H.R.H. The Prince of Wales

Colonel-in-Chief of
The Parachute Regiment

ST. JAMES'S PALACE

The capture and defence by the UK 6th Airborne Division of the bridges over the Caen Canal and the River Orne, on the western extreme of the British landing areas in Normandy, was one of the first and most decisive victories in the opening campaign of D-Day in June 1944. As such, this battle marked a defining moment for Britain's airborne forces.

"The Tale of Two bridges" recounts the story of this famous battle, told through the remarkable insights of the journal of Lieutenant Colonel Geoffrey Pine-Coffin DSO MC, Commanding Officer of 7th (Light Infantry) Parachute Battalion, at Pegasus Bridge. It includes tales of decisive leadership, outstanding courage and individual heroism.

"Pegasus Bridge", and the heroic actions of the men who fought there, have entered the folklore of the Parachute Regiment. The traditions they helped establish remain a focal point for the modern regiment, of which I am so immensely proud to be Colonel-in-Chief, and underpin the motto which remains ever true to this day: *Utrinque Paratus* — "Ready for Anything".

The Tale of Two Bridges

Colonel R.G. Pine-Coffin, DSO., MC.,
7th Bn (LI) The Parachute Regiment

Dedication

This book is the culmination of many years' work and it is written to commemorate the memory of all those who fought with 7 Para and paid the supreme sacrifice and whose names are recorded at the back of this book.

It is also dedicated to all who were wounded as well as those who took risks alongside their comrades, but were lucky enough to live through the battles - without whose help, and many memories recorded here, this publication would not have been possible.

Peter Pine-Coffin

Peter Pine-Coffin
Son of the late
Colonel R.G. Pine-Coffin, DSO, MC

> THIS PLAQUE COMMEMORATES
> LT COL R.G. PINE-COFFIN, DSO, MC, COMMANDING
> OFFICER AND 7TH BATTALION (L) THE PARACHUTE
> REGIMENT WHICH RELIEVED MAJOR HOWARD'S FORCE AT
> 0130 HRS ON 6TH JUNE 1944 AND HELD PEGASUS
> BRIDGE AND THE BENOUVILLE BRIDGEHEAD
> THROUGHOUT D.DAY DESPITE VERY HEAVY CASUALTIES

Author's Acknowledgements

I would like to take this opportunity to thank all the contributors for their kind permission to include all the various documents that have been used in this book.

I also place a heartfelt thanks to Peter Pine-Coffin for gathering all this information together and for collating all the documents and the permissions, and for the use of his father's diary, without which this book would not have been possible.

My thanks also go to my husband whose help and advice have, once again, been invaluable and also various friends, ex-paratroopers and other servicemen who will no doubt recognise their input and who willingly gave their time to explain to me the sometimes difficult military terminology.

My humble thanks go to all the armed forces and the 7th Parachute Battalion in particular whose devotion to duty during the Second World War has enabled me to enjoy a freedom which might not have been possible if the outcome had been different.

Barbara Maddox

Acknowledgements

This book could never have been written without the help and enthusiasm of many people, amongst them the Airborne Forces Museum and especially Alan Brown, Memorial Pegasus in Bénouville, with special thanks to Mark Worthington and his team at the Museum. To Tony Lycett special thanks for all his research, Eric Lancaster for his support and to Gordon and Joan Elliott for the provision of many anecdotes and photographs. Also Paul Aller, Ron Perry, Nick Archdale, The Imperial War Graves Commission, The Imperial War Museum. Darren Clarke, of KerryType, Midhurst who, with his team, has been very long suffering, helpful and above all else, like everyone who has been involved, enthusiastic for the project.

For the adaptation of the original diary I am deeply indebted to Barbara and Graham Maddox, who have toiled long and hard to produce this book. To my long-suffering neighbour Peter Brown, whose photography has been a great help with some of the research. And to my son Michael who chose the title and wrote the final paragraphs, also his mother (my wife), Jane, for her constant support and enthusiasm which has encouraged me all the way.

To all those who came home and lived to tell their stories, many of which appear within the book you are about to read, but above all to my late father, without whose diary the story could never have been told.

Peter Pine-Coffin

Prologue

The following pages contain a history of 7 Parachute Battalion. From its formation to training, in preparation for the D-Day landings and the eventual role they were to play, specifically in capturing the famous bridges at the Caen Canal and the River Orne.

Many stories and films depict the subject, and are entertaining and informative. However, this book is different in as much that this story will, in the main, be told from the actual diaries and photographs of the Commanding Officer and the memoirs of some of the men who served under him.

The accounts from the men show how clearly they revered their Commanding Officer and how they held him in great esteem, many owing their lives to him and he to them. Many of these accounts are shot through with a humour which can only be described as quintessentially British. Indeed, as you read them, you cannot fail to be as moved and amused as I was when I first read them.

I agreed to be the author of this work because these very personal accounts have never seen the light of day and contain a story that should be told, if only to remind us of what tragic circumstances occur in times of war and of the scars inflicted, many of which never heal.

I feel very honoured to be the voice of these men and in this small way I hope to pay tribute to a few of the so many who fought for the freedom that I have, so that I can bring their words to you.

I wish that all these men were still here, but time has passed and few are left. Those who are are often reluctant to tell their stories, or think that perhaps, generations on, no-one is interested, or that this is a subject which is already well known.

I hope in these pages, to redress these issues, to tell the untold story of 'The Tale of Two Bridges', so that we may see the human side of war, rather than having to believe what we are told through official accounts and films.

War is inhuman, no-one can deny that, and to say otherwise is misleading. People - humans - become the enemy, the Germans, the Boche. The instruments of war become Tanks, 'Planes etc. The Wounded, Pilots etc. Perhaps this de-humanisation is the only way man can cope with killing man. Maybe this is why we are developing remote controlled weapons, so that mankind doesn't have to look man in the eye to kill him.

The men of 7 Para had a job to do, and against all odds they did it well. Many others fought and died for freedom, but this book is to tell the untold story of the 7 Paras.

Let us hope that we may never have to call on their descendants to fulfil again the roles of their brave and gallant forefathers.

Through these pages I hope to have fulfilled the wishes of Geoffrey Pine-Coffin, that this untold story of the Battalion be told.

Barbara Maddox

NB: Quotes in this book that appear in **bold** type are taken directly from the diaries of Geoffrey Pine-Coffin, those in plain type are my adaptations of entries in the diaries, whilst those in *italics* are taken from the officers and men who fought in the battles. Some of the authors' identities have been lost over a period of time. Their contribution - from whoever they may be - is greatly appreciated.

The Tale of Two Bridges

Every Man an Emperor

What manner of men are these who wear the maroon beret?

They are, firstly, all volunteers and are then toughened by hard physical training. As a result they have that infectious optimism and that offensive eagerness which comes from physical well being.

They have jumped from the air and by so doing have conquered fear. Their duty lies in the van of battle: they are proud of their honour and have never failed in any task.

They have the highest standards in all things, whether it be skill in battle or smartness in execution of all peacetime duties. They have shown themselves to be tenacious and determined in defence as they are courageous in attack.

They are, in fact, men apart.

Monty wishes the men good luck

Photo: Airborne Forces Museum

WAR DECLARED

At noon on Sunday September 3rd 1939 Prime Minister Neville Chamberlain announced in the House of Commons, "This country is now at war with Germany," the speech took just two minutes to make.

In the evening the King made a broadcast to the Commonwealth, "We can only do right as we see right, and we reverently commit our cause to God."

The French Government made its declaration from Paris at 5pm also on September 3rd.

On September 4th Winston Churchill, after a break of 25 years, was again 1st Lord of the Admiralty and joined a small war cabinet.

By September 30th the world had sorted out its various positions with regard to the outbreak of war in Europe, with the USA taking the expected stance of neutrality.

On Wednesday May 10th Neville Chamberlain resigned after a vote of no confidence after the British debacle in Norway. Leo Amery and Sir Roger Keyes joined forces over the operational bungling in Norway. The Prime Minister appealed for Tory loyalty, a vote was taken: 281 for and 200 against - 41 Tories voted against Mr Chamberlain and 60 abstained.

The rebels refused any co-operation with the Government unless Labour and Liberals were included. Labour wouldn't co-operate unless Chamberlain resigned. Chamberlain said he would, in favour of Lord Halifax, the Foreign Secretary, Labour still wouldn't have it, and so in the end it had to be Winston Churchill.

The French were forced to sign their surrender on Saturday June 22nd 1940. By June 25th the German occupation of France had begun. And so it remained until the liberation started on June 6th 1944 at the Pegasus Bridge, which was the first area of France to be recaptured by the allies on what was known as **D-DAY**.

Appointments - Normandy

Bn HQ
CO	Lt Col Pine-Coffin
2 I/C	Maj Steel-Baume
Adjt	Capt Coppin
MO	Capts Young/Wagstaffe
Med	Cpl Bartle
Padre	Capt Parry
RSM	RSM Johnson
APTC	S/I Williams
APTC	S/I Farlow
Prov Sgt	Sgt Masterman
Prov Cpl	Cpl Holmes
Ord Room Sgt	Sgt Dickens
Ord Room Cpl	Cpl Aller

HQ Coy
OC Coy	Maj Tullis
Admn Capt	Capt Went
CSM	CSM Hutchins
CQMS	CQMS Midlane

Int Sec
IO	Lt Mills
Int Sgt	Sgt Lowrie

Sig Pl
SO	Lt Theobald

Mort Pl
Pl Comd	Lt Archdale
Pl Sgt	Sgt Beech
Det Comd	Sgt Fricker
Det Comd	Sgt Roberts

MMG Pl
Bde MMG Offr	Lt Bowler
Pl Comd	Lt Hill
Pl Sgt	Sgt Sperrell
Sec Comd	Sgt French
Sec Comd	Sgt Cope

AA & A/Tk Pl
Pl Comd	Lt Rogers
Pl Sgt	Sgt Warwick

Admn Pl
QM	Capt Fortnum
RQMS	RQMS Cowan
Cook Sgt	Sgt Woods
Arm Sgt	Sgt Thompson
Post Cpl	L/C Edwards

'A' Coy
OC Coy	Maj Taylor
2 I/C	Capt Webber
CSM	CSM Leverton
CQMS	CQMS Semple
Runner	Pte Humble

No 1 Pl
Pl Comd	Lt Temple
Pl Sgt	Sgt Villiers
Sec Comd	Sgt Harris
Sec Comd	Sgt Kingston
Sec Comd	Sgt Kempster

No 2 Pl
Pl Comd	Lt Bowyer
Pl Sgt	Sgt Clarke
Sec Comd	Sgt Fiddler
Sec Comd	Sgt Richard
Sec Comd	Sgt Case

No 3 Pl
Pl Comd	Lt Hunter
Pl Sgt	Sgt McCullough
Sec Comd	Sgt Aitkenhead
Sec Comd	Sgt McCauley
Sec Comd	Sgt Wyse

'B' Coy
OC Coy	Maj Neale
2 I/C	Capt Braithwaite
CSM	CSM Durbin
CQMS	CQMS Bush
Runner	Pte Cornell

No 4 Pl
Pl Comd	Lt Farr
Pl Sgt	Sgt Lucas
Sec Comd	Sgt Bettle
Sec Comd	Sgt Barnett
Sec Comd	Sgt Baldwin

No 5 Pl
Pl Comd	Lt Poole
Pl Sgt	Sgt Prentice
Sec Comd	Sgt Bethell
Sec Comd	Sgt Harper
Sec Comd	Sgt McCambridge

No 6 Pl
Pl Comd	Lt Thomas
Pl Sgt	Sgt Amey
Sec Comd	Sgt Lock
Sec Comd	Sgt Godbold

'C' Coy
OC Coy	Maj Bartlett
2 I/C	Capt Keene
CSM	CSM Martin
CQMS	CQMS Savill
Runner	Pte Gay

No 7 Pl
Pl Comd	Lt Parrish
Pl Sgt	Sgt French
Sec Comd	Sgt Fear
Sec Comd	Sgt Irwin
Sec Comd	Sgt Conway

No 8 Pl
Pl Comd	Lt Woodman
Pl Sgt	Sgt Bessant
Sec Comd	Sgt Powell
Sec Comd	Sgt Wilkes
Sec Comd	Sgt Tandy

No 9 Pl
Pl Comd	Lt Atkinson
Pl Sgt	Sgt Lake
Sec Comd	Sgt Blakeway
Sec Comd	Sgt Wynstanley

The Tale of Two Bridges

Order of Battle
6th Airborne Division

General Officer Commanding
Major General R.N. Gale, DSO, OBE, MC

Divisional HQ
CRA	Norris
CRE	Lowman
Div Sigs	Tew
CRASC	Lovegrove
ADMS	McEwan
ADOS	Fielding
CREME	Powditch
SCF	Hales
Recce Rgt	Stuart

5th Parachute Brigade
Brigadier J.H.H. Poett, DSO
7 Para Bn	Pine-Coffin
12th Para Bn	Johnson
13th Para Bn	Luard

212 A/L Lt Bty RA
4 L/A Tk Bty RA
591 Para Sqn RE
225 Para Fd Amb

Coup-de-Main Group
D Coy 2nd Oxf & Bucks
B Coy 2nd Oxf & Bucks
(2 platoons)
Detachment 249 Fd Coy RE

Divisional Troops
Armd Recce Regt Gp
53 A/L Lt Regt RA
22 Indep Para Coy
249 Fd Coy RE
286 Fd Park Coy RE
716 Coy RASC
398 Coy RASC
63 Coy RASC
Ord Fd Pks
Div Signals
REME wkshops
317 Fd Security Sec
Div Pro Coy
No 1 Wing
No 2 Wing Gp Regt

3rd Parachute Brigade
Brigadier S.J.L. Hill, DSO, MC
8th Para Bn	Pearson
9th Para Bn	Otway
1st Can Para Bn	Bradbrooke

211 A/L Lt Bty RA
3 A/LA Tk Bty RA
3 Para Sqn RE
224 Para Fd Amb

6th Airlanding Brigade
Brigadier Hon
H. Kindersley
1st Bn Ulster Rifles	R Carson
2nd Bn Ox&Bucks	C Roberts
12th Bn Devons	I Stevens

1st Special Service Commando Brigade
(Came under command of the Division after linking up at the Orne Canal Bridge)
Brigadier The Lord Lovat, DSO, MC
No 3 Army CDO	Young
No 4 Army CDO	Dawson
No 6 CDO	Mills, Roberts
No 45 Royal Marines	Ries
The French CDO	Keiffer - 1er Bn Fusiliers Marins

2 Troops (No 1 & 8) in strength about 177 att to No 4 Army CDO

Chapter One

'Go To It'
attributed to General (Windy) Gale

The idea of a human descending to earth, suspended by a pocket of air, contained under a piece of material to which strings are attached to keep open a canopy and provide a means for a human to hold onto was, like many inventions, first thought of by Leonardo de Vinci (1452-1519). The first man to test this idea was L.S. Lenormand of France, who used it to descend from a high tower in 1783.

A few years later, in 1797, Andre Garnervin made a successful descent from a hot air balloon. Thereafter many more descents were made, and by the French in particular. From these beginnings, parachuting became popular public entertainment during the nineteenth century.

During the years of the Second World War, Adolf Hitler decided to form a parachute division; the men were trained and then sent to Crete in the Greek Islands (1941), which led to disastrous results. Many men were killed, so many in fact that Herr Hitler decided that it wasn't such a good idea after all and never used them again.

Meanwhile, here in Britain, Winston Churchill had been watching these results from afar and realised the potential of the parachute and decided to form a parachute regiment in Britain.

It was to be called The 6th Airborne Division under the command of Major General R.N. Gale, DSO, OBE, MC (see breakdown of the Order of Battle, opposite).

May 11th had seen the Airborne Forces Depot and Development Centre officially established, under the command of Brigadier Edward Flavell, at Hardwick Hall, situated near to Number 1 Parachute Training Centre at Ringway near Manchester.

The Development Centre was established separately at Amesbury Abbey in Wiltshire under the command of Lieutenant Colonel J.G. Squirrell. It was charged with the task of developing new equipment for the airborne forces.

The Tale of Two Bridges

The year of 1943 and the spring of 1944 saw the Brigade going through intensive training. This is a brief history of the formation of the 6th Airborne Division and the following role of the 7th Parachute Battalion (LI) and its Commanding Officer, Lt. Col. R. Geoffrey Pine-Coffin, DSO, MC, within that Division.

One of the soldiers describes joining the 7th Battalion:
"*In the winter of 1943 (after transfer from the Durham Light Infantry), I completed a rigorous physical evaluation at Hardwick Hall, Chesterfield, and obtained my Parachute qualification at Ringway, Manchester, before joining 7th Battalion (LI). The Battalion's Commanding Officer was Colonel Pine-Coffin. I thought at the time what a peculiar name.*" This description comes from Eric (Bill) Sykes.

Another, Bob Tanner, explains how he came to join the forces:
"*Doing anything to earn a penny, joining the ARP as a messenger, later a warden, then the Army. Went to Catterick Camp, the train seemed to go on and on. I thought any minute we would end up in the sea, I didn't realise England was so big. The Royal Tank Regiment, passing out as a driver/mechanic on Churchills, Valentines, Crusaders and Cromwells, the different lorries, and the biggest of all the Diamond 'T' Tank Transporter. In and around Yorkshire and the Midlands; and the best memory of them all then, and still is, the kindness shown by the people of these places, to me, a stranger, really fascinated by the way they spoke. Quite a few miserable buggers down here could learn a lot from these people.*

Then one day some Bods came round asking for volunteers - a much dreaded word in the forces. In for a penny in for a pound.

Hardwick.... Who could forget it, the training, the torture, getting through it all, how? Was it pride, stubbornness, don't suppose I'll ever know. Then Ringway, The dear old Whitley... Bessy the Balloon, qualifying to join the finest bunch of men anyone could meet, the privilege of joining the 7 Parachute Battalion, Colonel Pine-Coffin, DSO, MC, what a man, set us all a high standard by his coolness and courage. The constant exercises, practice jumps, forced marches and map readings, firing all manner of weapons, for the big job that was to come."

That last description shows us that many of these men had never been away from their towns, villages or even their families before.

Richard Todd, the film actor, writes: *"In May 1943, I successfully passed my Parachute training course and tests, did my seven qualifying drops, was taken on the strength of the Seventh Battalion (LI) The Parachute Regiment, and reported to the Battalion HQ at Bulford near Salisbury.*

As soon as I met him I knew that I was very fortunate to be in a Battalion commanded by Lt. Col. R.G. Pine-Coffin, DSO, MC. Tall, lean and tough, with long-nosed humorous features and quizzical, crinkled eyes, he was the quintessential military leader. A Devonian (a Pine-Coffin had been with me at my prep school in Exeter), he had been one of the finest senior officers to volunteer for parachute duties, and was a man of extraordinary bravery, but still a caring, wise Commander whose planning always took in the welfare of his men. Quiet spoken and almost gentle in his manner, there was no tough guy swagger from Geoffrey Pine-Coffin.

Capt Richard ('Sweeney') Todd 'B' Echelon

During the twelve months preceding D-Day 6th of June 1944, he forged the 7th (LI) Parachute Battalion into a magnificent fighting unit, supremely trained and prepared for the crucial role it was to play in the invasion of Normandy. The pride and bond that he instilled into his men exists today amongst those of us still alive, together with great affection for his memory."

Another, Syd Mundy, describes his time at Hardwick Hall as: *"A toughening up Depot, one did not do any parachute training there, as such, but was put through a physically demanding programme of severe physical tests, designed to toughen up each potential paratrooper.*

No walking was allowed in the Depot, and from time to time, once arrived, everywhere had to be at the double (run), even if one was going out in the evening you had to run as far as the gate before you started walking. The course lasted for about four weeks, at the end of which you had to pass a series of tests before moving on to actual

The Tale of Two Bridges

parachute training. The tests were a final weeding out process, if you failed just one, that was it, Return To Unit (RTU). Included in the passing out tests were all the likes of jumping a 9ft (2.8m) wide ditch of water whilst wearing full battle order and carrying a rifle. One three-minute round of milling in a boxing ring in which you had to endeavour to knock the stuffing out of your opponent, complete an assault course 1 1/2 miles long (at times under fire from live ammunition) and, one of the toughest, a 10-mile (16km) forced march - a combination of marching and running, which had to be completed in between 1 hour 20 - 1 hour 35. In our Platoon it was a Lieutenant Essex-Lopreski, a Medical Officer, who for the last few miles kept mumbling to himself 'Oh God, tell them to stop, tell them to walk'. With a hand from a couple of us, he made it back to the depot with the rest of the Platoon."

Training was hard for these men, even for officers, as one here describes his days at Hardwick. His recurring nightmare is of the tunnels there:

"As an officer leading a section of five or six men I had, in my fortnight at Hardwick, to go through the tunnels at least five or six times, all the time the fear growing heavier on my shoulders. So much so that for one fleeting instance on my last day, when ordered by the APTC Sergeant to 'Tek your bloody men through agen Sir', I almost gave up and told him what he could do with his tunnels. The tunnels were a hated feature at Hardwick. Thank God I didn't. I wanted to be in the Regiment too much to be RTU'd. So what were the tunnels? They came immediately after one of the nastier water obstacles. One of these bloody obstacles that no matter how fit you were, how fast you could run, how far you could jump, or how well you could hang on to a rope, you inevitably finished up to your waist in ice cold water, dirty, slime ridden, Derbyshire water. All you could see as you approached at the double was, in front of you, apparently a highly organised rabbit warren. The ground, very crumbly sandstone, sloped down to six or seven very even openings disappearing into the earth. Above these holes were woven hurdles, to the depth of a couple of feet were rough turfs and on top of those clods of loose earth and sandstone. So all you saw, virtually, were seven holes gaping into an awful

frightening unknown of blackness. Onto your belly, two feet inside you were in pitch darkness. With your pack on your back there was just enough room to edge along, bringing down, in the darkness, sand and earth into your eyes and mouth."

These are some of the thoughts and experiences of a few of the men who served in 7 Para, from joining up to training, serving and fighting.

"The 7th of November 1942 was the day the Battalion was born and to describe very briefly its growth and development. Prior to this date it had existed as the 10th Battalion, Somerset Light Infantry Commanded by Lt. Col. K.G.G. Dennys.

The Battalion was turned over to Parachuting as a formed body and those who wished to do so were given the chance to drop out; others including the CO were weeded out by the medical board. Nearly 70% of the original Battalion survived the turnover and became the 7th Battalion of the Parachute Regiment.

The conversion in this way of an existing Battalion was an excellent idea as no time had to be spent in setting up the machinery of administration thus avoiding many of the teething problems which had hampered the early days of the 1st Parachute Brigade in 1941. The gaps in the various ranks were filled by parachute volunteers from various Light Infantry and Rifle Regiments and the Battalion took the title of 7th Battalion (LI) The Parachute Regiment. It was given permission at the same time to wear a green diamond as a backing for the cap badge on the maroon beret, and ever since it has been possible to recognise a member of the Battalion by this distinction.

The Battalion was naturally drawn on freely, not only for advice on matters parachuting, but also for personnel. Many first class officers and other ranks left at this stage to assume appointments within the Brigade. Their loss was a heavy blow to the Battalion, but the resulting gain to the Brigade as a whole was an asset to everyone including the Battalion. It was a period of give and take but, under the circumstances the emphasis, was very definitely on the 'give' as far as the Battalion was concerned.

The training of 5 Brigade followed much the same lines as that of 3 Brigade and the rest of the Division; there was a very noticeable spirit of competition between the two Brigades. The Battalion had a big advantage by having served in both of them and practically everyone knew personally the members not only of their own Brigade but that of the other one as well.

After completing its parachute training at Ringway, near Manchester, the Battalion moved to Gordon Barracks, Bulford, where it formed part of the 3rd Parachute Brigade, commanded by Brig. S.J.L. Hill, DSO, MC, and was carefully trained in the somewhat general lines that were necessary at that time. No-one could foresee what they would be called upon to do, but when the call came there must be no failure from lack of preliminary training."

Part of the training was 'Bessie the Balloon':

"No-one liked Bessie very much as she was silent and the basket used to swing in the wind. Also, as there was no slip stream, you got a fall of about 100 feet before your chute opened (which it did with a crack like a whip). You definitely got a falling sensation. She was good for beginners though as there was practically no swinging and everyone landed about the same spot. An instructor used to stand near this spot with a megaphone and talk to the men as they came down."

The Bessie experience is related by another parachutist in training:

"There was a slight movement, a dipping and a lifting, a slight tugging and letting go. It reminded one of a fishermen's float on the surface of the water, going with the swell and ripple of the river's current, but not quite able to break free.

It was a dark night, a very, very dark night. There were no lights visible wherever one looked.

Eight men stood in this confined space, they had to stand close together. Closer than they would have stood had there been more room, they knew each other, but only with the experience of three weeks. Tension was in the air, it was not directed against each other, but against the apprehension of what they were about to do, the ten-

The Tale of Two Bridges

sion and apprehension did not amount to fear, their training thus far had instilled a lot of confidence, but this was the moment of truth. Things could go wrong, they had gone wrong before, but not to these men, always someone else. Nevertheless, they knew that not very far away ambulances were on standby for any casualties and trained crews were with them. The presence of these vehicles, strangely, gave them some confidence as they had been taught to think positively and they would give the crews the thumbs up sign when they met up later.

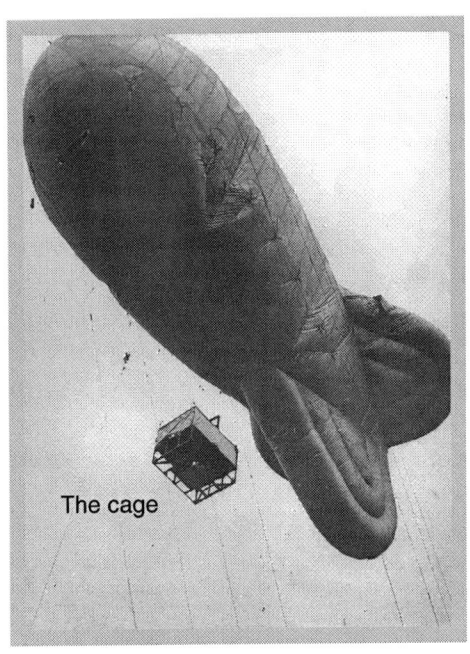

The cage

'Bessie' the barrage balloon

They didn't talk very much and if it had been daylight the grins would have seemed a little forced and unnatural. Only one man seemed to be really at ease with the situation and he stood at the rear of the group, he was there to see them on their way and all being well would meet up later.

The slight movement that they had been experiencing changed slightly, it was still there, but there was a subtle alteration in its nature. The violin strings of their nerves tightened up a notch, they knew they had arrived at their start point and it was time to go.

No. 1 stepped one pace forward smartly and immediately dropped like a stone, it was a heart-stopping moment. He could feel himself falling and could only wait, he could not control his destiny any longer. It was only seconds when he felt that welcome wiggling tug at his shoulders, then a crack, identical but much louder than when his mother used to shake the bedsheets after taking them down from the washing line. Immediately he heard that sound he decelerated sharply and his descent was much more leisurely and he was filled with relief and satisfaction. The confined space he had just left was a flimsy canvas surrounded cage slung under Bessie the barrage balloon which had been allowed to rise to 700 feet. The seven other men still had to jump, but while he wished them a safe landing, he still had to prepare for his own landing on terra firma. The landing was responsible for most of the accidents which occurred, ranging from sprains to broken limbs, but in numbers they were quite rare. This particular landing by No. 1 was a catastrophe in technical terms, he might well never have had any training, he had no idea how far he had to go or in which direction he was heading and he was hit by Mother Earth without any warning and with even less gentleness, he was flung onto his back and was dazed by the blow to the back of his head. Now that he was safely down, he rolled up his parachute and, feeling ten feet tall, he made his way to the edge of the drop zone. That was his fifth jump, three more and he could get his wings and put the red beret on his head." [The author may well have jumped at a later date, which explains why the balloon basket was larger than the original.]

"The training policy was laid down by Major General R.H. Gale, Commander of the 6th Airborne Division, and was carefully explained to all ranks so that each officer and man knew the reason for every exercise he was called upon to do. Even the most unobservant could not fail to notice that he was part of a Division which was growing rapidly and, at the same time, was one that was going to live up to its motto 'Go To It'.

There was a life and energy about every phase of life. Everyone put all they knew into everything they did, whether it was working or playing, and as a result a splen-

Major General R.N. Gale, DSO., OBE., MC.
Photo: Airborne Forces Museum

did spirit of comradeship developed automatically throughout the Division.

The Battalion, for its part, always possessed a distinct spirit of its own, just as some individuals have a pronounced personality. No-one has ever been able to describe just what this spirit is and no attempt will be made here, suffice to say that it exists to a marked degree and that it grew stronger as time went on.

In July 1943 Brigadier J.H.N. Poett joined the Division and was charged with the job of forming and training a brand new Brigade, to be known as the 5th Parachute Brigade. His job was formidable and time was not unlimited; but he had to get results and he had to get them quickly. One of his first steps was to ask General Gale to give him one Battalion which was already a going concern which he could use as a nucleus. The 7th Battalion was selected for this job and joined the 5th Brigade the same month and has served in it through all the events described in this account.

Brigadier Poett receives his DSO from General Omar Bradley

Photo: Airborne Forces Museum

The Tale of Two Bridges

In February 1944, Lt. Col. H.N. Barlow, OBE, who commanded the Battalion, was transferred to the 1st Airborne Division as Deputy Commander of the 1st Airlanding Brigade, in which capacity he was unhappily killed at Arnhem. The Battalion owes much to the steady work put in by Barlow, who made no secret of the fact that he would much have preferred to have gone to war in command of the men that he himself had trained. Command of the Battalion passed to myself. I had joined the Battalion some three months previously from 1st Airborne Division and was then Second-in-Command."

At this juncture the following quotation from the 'History of the 7 Parachute Battalion' takes up the story:

"1944 saw intensified special training for the invasion of the continent. Brigade drops were carried out by day and night. Early in 1944 the Battalion carried out its first drops as a complete unit. On 26th February Lt. Col. Barlow was appointed Deputy Commander 1st Air Landing Brigade and was succeeded in command of the Battalion by Lt. Col. R.G. Pine-Coffin. During March training in street fighting was carried out in bombed areas of Southampton. Here a serious accident occurred in which Sgt. Stenner was killed and Lieutenants J.H. Loch and R. Fleming were seriously injured."

"The Battalion was practically ready for action so the training took the form of keeping the edge sharp and the introduction of improvements of method here and there. The whole Division was ready for action about this time and a considerable number of large-scale exercises were carried out, many of them including a parachute descent. It was obvious that during these exercises the Brigades and Battalions were being weighed up against one another and it was a trying time for Commanders lest some error of judgement on their part or some slackness by any of their subordinates should prejudice the chances of their commands when the selection of the real jobs was being made. The first Airborne Division - veterans of North Africa and Italy - were also in England ready for further action, so it was a matter of great anxiety within the Division whether their reputation would make them an automatic choice for employment within that Division. The 6th Airborne Division could not compete against this reputation because they still had to win their spurs. Eventually the two Divisions were pitted against each other in the biggest exercise of airborne troops ever held in the country. The Corps Commander, Lieutenant General F.A.M. Browning, DSO, when speaking to a gathering of officers and senior NCOs at Bulford, said that he expected this clash to be a 'hairy affair'. It was. Both sides were on their toes and the stakes were very high; it was fought out in a friendly but keen spirit in the peaceful Oxfordshire countryside."

The Commanding Officer addressing the Battalion before they moved off for the exercise pointed out the great importance of the occasion, he called for an extra special effort from everyone and he got it too. The Battalion had the honour of being specially named by General Gale at his conference, after the exercise, for its alertness in beating off an early morning attack on the last day and felt that it was in a good position for getting a critical job.

During the next few weeks it was vital not to undermine this good position by any thoughtless lapse on the part of any individual member of the Battalion. Special attention was paid to all matters of discipline and, in order to avoid a large number of minor charges appearing on the conduct sheets, a special period known as 'Ginger Week' was instituted. A Ginger Week was a conscious effort by the whole Battalion to ginger itself up for a period of seven days. No single infringement of the smallest regulation was allowed to pass unnoticed and offenders were assembled daily in the square to be drilled till they sweated. The whole week was a period of considerable amusement and was appreciated even by those who were unlucky enough to find themselves 'Gingered'.

All this time it was noticeable that something more than mere training was afoot. More and more officers would lock themselves away in their rooms of an evening and work late into the night, but refuse to tell others what they were working on. These were the ones who had been admitted to the select band who held a green ticket, giving them free entry into a small house tucked away behind Divisional Headquarters, near Netheraven. This house, despite its innocent appearance, contained one of the most carefully guarded secrets in the world. In it was not only the complete plan of action for

The Tale of Two Bridges

the airborne troops in the coming invasion, but also all the apparatus for demonstrating this plan in the most minute detail. The apparatus was a wonder in itself and was a revelation to all who saw it of the completeness of the Allied Intelligence.

There were as many maps as would be required. All of them accurate, up to the minute aerial photographs of all sizes covering the entire area from every angle and height; volumes of information reports from which could be gleaned even the names of civil officials of tiny villages and, finally, models of the area which were so accurate that distances and angles could be measured from them with confidence.

All this was being devised to make the 7th Battalion's task as easy, under the circumstances, as possible.

Some small sections of the map opposite have been included in the text to indicate the areas mentioned in the narrative in relationship to the bridges

The Tale of Two Bridges

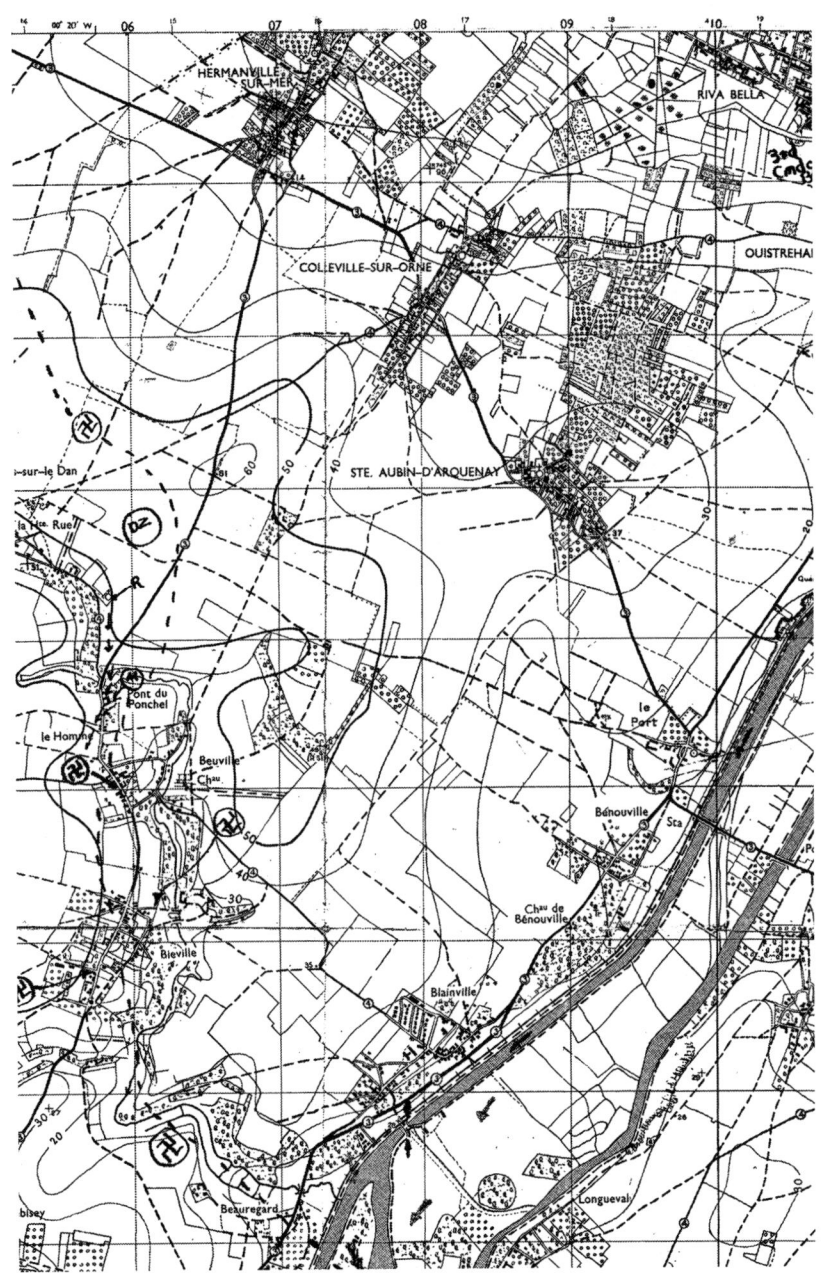

Part of an original official map of the area
Map: Airborne Forces Museum

Chapter Two

The Task

The 7 Parachute Battalion's task was to seize the bridges of the Caen Canal and the River Orne at Bénouville and Ranville.

"As this account deals only with the experiences of the Battalion it is not prepared to go, at any length, into the Divisional plan as a whole. It will only be referred to in outline."

There has already been numerous mentions of the sea landings for the D-Day offensives, but as no unit of the 6th Airborne was involved it is not relevant here to involve them. What is important to note is that the 6th Airborne Division included the 5th Parachute Brigade, composed of 7 (LI), 12th and 13th Parachute Battalions.

"The eastern edge of the Allied bridgehead was bounded by the Caen Canal which runs between Ouistreham, on the coast, and the town from which it takes its name; parallel to this canal, and four hundred yards to the east of it, runs the River Orne. One road crosses these two water obstacles and it does so at right angles from the little village of Bénouville, crossing the canal by a swing bridge, pivoted at the centre. Bénouville is about midway between Ouistreham and Caen.

The 6th Airborne Division was to land on or after midnight on the night before D-Day and to seize both of these bridges and hold them. It would thus fulfil the dual role of safeguarding the Allied left flank and preserving the bridges for Allied use at a later date.

The seizure of the bridges intact was very desirable, but not absolutely vital. General Gale planned to get them by surprise with a coup-de-main force to be landed in gliders right on the bridges themselves and thirty minutes before the main parachute landing.

Simultaneously with the arrival of the coup-de-main party a small number of parachutists were to land on the main dropping zone (DZ), with guide lights and other aids to hasten the forming up of the remainder of the parachutists when they landed.

The main drop was timed for 0050hrs and was to be followed a few hours later by a small number of essential gliders. The main glider element was to come in at noon the following day.

The Battalion was selected for the job of holding the bridges themselves and, with them, the west flank of the Divisional Bridgehead until such time as the seaborne troops closed the gap. It also had the subsidiary job of establishing contact with these seaborne troops. The coup-de-main party, which consisted of some seventy members of the 2nd Battalion Oxford and Buck's under the command of Major J. Howard, was to come under the command of the Battalion as soon as it had done its job.

The Battalion was to establish a bridgehead west of the canal, whether or not the bridges had been blown. In addition, a battery position was to be neutralised and occupied.

First contact with the seaborne troops was to be expected about 11am on D-Day and was to be with No. 2 Commando Brigade under Brigadier Lord Lovat, DSO, MC. Lovat's force was to cross the bridges and enter the Divisional Bridgehead, where it came under the command of the Division. It would, however, be several hours ahead of the bulk of the troops as its orders were to force its way through somehow and not wait for the main forces, whose advance was to be systematic and therefore slower. These main forces were expected to reach the canal by about 5pm and, until they arrived, the holding off of all attacks and the Divisional Bridgehead from the west would fall wholly on the Battalion and the coup-de-main force. The Battalion had been given a plum job, but the responsibility was a very heavy one."

Only the officers knew this sequence of events, but another of the men of 7 Para has memories both good and bad leading up to this planned invasion. His recollections of the final exercise the night before they were to jump are as follows:

"We were all outside the billet at Bulford watching some poor devil whose parachute had gone over the tail plane of the Dakota, relieved to hear that he had successfully pulled in (even though he belonged to the Provo Staff). Our jump next day had one refusal, felt sorry for fellow. Remember remark by CO Colonel Pine-Coffin to our

Major Fraser regarding 7th getting plum job. This was while being briefed in model hut. Next memory was take off, someone started singing, this had a good effect of relaxing everyone, right up to the time for hook up."

On June 1st, according to Pine-Coffin: **"The Battalion left Bulford and moved to its transit camp at Tilshead, where it was sealed in with elaborate precautions to prevent exit from, or unauthorised entry into, the camp.** A briefing room was set up in the camp in which the intelligence section, under Lieutenant Mills, worked day and night, preparing models and displaying the photographs and other exhibits to the best advantage and in making large-scale maps for use at the Battalion briefing.

Major Frank Fraser

In a parachute operation it is of vital importance for everyone to know the plan as a whole, as anyone may well be dropped in the wrong spot and end up fighting in some Company, or even a Battalion, other than his own.

There is, however, a tendency for a man to concentrate on his own particular job and only give half of his attention to other people's. Briefing had to be done extremely thoroughly and a mass of detail had to be absorbed.

The entire Battalion was assembled in a suitable place, actually the Garrison Cinema, and there the Commanding Officer outlined the Divisional and Brigade plans, but was careful not to mention which unit was to do any particular job. Lieutenant Mills then took the stage and described the topography of the area, information of the known and suspected enemy positions in it, probable attitudes of the civilians and a number of relevant points. The Battalion then broke for a smoke and a chat and finally I took the stage once more, but this time in a silence that was almost overpowering. With the aid of a large-scale map I pointed out which of the roles had been allotted to the Battalion and then ran through the Battalion plan in outline, again being careful not to name any specific Company at any time.

During the remaining days at Tilshead the briefing room was allotted to companies and the various Commanders briefed their

The Tale of Two Bridges

men in their own particular jobs with the comforting knowledge that the general plan was already known and the men could safely be allowed to concentrate on their own particular job.

The Company Commanders had been issued with their green tickets two days before going to Tilshead and had been fully briefed by the CO in the Divisional briefing house.

The briefing room was only a small hut of limited capacity, but by careful allocation and a strict 'No Smoking' rule every soldier had, at least, three separate hours in there with his own officer and access to every photograph and model.

The Battalion plan had to be a double one because no-one could say whether or not the bridges would be captured, or, if they were captured, whether they would be blown or not. In either event though the main landing was to be at 0050hrs on the night before D-Day. And the Battalion rendezvous (RV) was to be a feature at the west end of the DZ.

If the main party had managed to get the bridges intact Howard was to signal this success by blowing Victory Vs on a whistle and firing from a Bren, and the Battalion would double across both and go straight into its pre-arranged positions to the west of the canal. This was the ideal plan, but it seemed too good to hope for.

In the more complicated event of the bridges not having been captured or if they had been blown, or alternatively if only one had been captured or only one blown, the crossing of the two water obstacles at night would present quite as big a problem as one wanted. There would, of course, be Germans about the place, intent on making it even more difficult. This seemed a very likely thing to happen, so boating equipment was to be carried.

Fifty-two RAF-type inflatable dinghies, two folding recce boats and long lengths of rope had somehow to be added to the normal equipment which would be carried, and a parachutist carries everything on his back, because he has no transport at first.

Two fairly similar water obstacles exist at Countess Weare, near Exeter, and the Battalion spent five very pleasant days down there practising crossings by day and night with this type of equipment. No one except myself knew, at that time, the signifi-

The Tale of Two Bridges

cance of this training, but everyone realised that it was of more than usual importance and got down to it in earnest, and at the end of the period the crossing of each obstacle was only a matter of minutes.

It would be a different problem though in Normandy and the capture of the bridges intact was very desirable from the Battalion's point of view.

Tilshead had been the permanent barracks of the 8th Parachute Battalion and so was considerably more comfortable than the temporary camps in which the other units were sealed. It had the disadvantage though of being a long way from the airfield at Fairford in Gloucestershire, which was the one from which the Battalion was to take off. Many snags can arise on a long road trip with a column of vehicles, so a tented camp was erected in a secluded wood clearing about two miles from the airport itself.

The Battalion was to start from Tilshead early in the morning and arrive to rest for as much time as was available in this halting place, from which it could reach the airfield without fear of breakdown or hold ups.

On June 3rd all preparations were made for an early start to take place the following morning, because the Cipher signal had been received stating that D-Day would be the 5th of June. In the early evening, though, another signal came in announcing postponement of twenty-four hours. This meant another comfortable night, but most members of the Battalion found it an odd sensation to lie in a peaceful bed knowing that the following night, at the same time, they would be descending behind enemy lines on a parachute.

On 5th June the Battalion moved off as arranged, and arrived at the halting camp in time for a hot mid-day meal. The next couple of hours or so were spent on the airfield itself where there was much to be done. Parachutes were drawn and harnesses adjusted carefully to fit over the equipment which would be worn, aircraft were examined and the pilots and aircrews met for the first time. These things are matters which cannot be rushed for obvious reasons and it was late afternoon before the Battalion returned to their camp for as much sleep as could be filled in."

At this time Bill Elvin was a Private in 4 Platoon, 'B' Company, 7th Battalion (LI), this is how his war started:

"I suppose that my D-Day escapade started in the late afternoon of the 5th of June when we boarded trucks at our concentration area on Salisbury Plain to go to the aerodrome at Fairford. As our convoy of trucks passed through the English countryside, there were groups of people in the villages who waved us farewell. Some of the women were in tears as if they guessed that something big was about to begin.

We arrived at Fairford in the early evening and were taken to our planes which were four-engined Stirlings. Twenty Paras were allotted to each plane and all our unit was unloaded. We then had parachutes issued and all this took time, it was getting dark by the time we were ready, we looked like a lot of little Michelin men, I was carrying as much equipment in weight as I weighed myself."

Bill Elvin

While all this issuing of equipment was going on, and the hustle and bustle of various troops arriving and planes and crews being got ready, Brigadier Poett visited the Battalion:

"He went round chatting informally to anyone he found. His visit was immensely appreciated by everyone. The fact that he had spent the whole afternoon and evening motoring round the various camps was freely commented upon. He had arranged to jump with the advanced party and would take off and jump thirty minutes before us. He could have had no rest himself all day. During his visit he was called upon to make a decision. Lieutenant Lewendon, Commander of number 7 Platoon, had developed a boil on his chest which, it was thought, might be irritated by his parachute harness; should

Lt 'Butch' Lewendon

The Tale of Two Bridges

he be allowed to jump or should he be replaced. The Medical Officer, Captain A. Young, RAMC, thought he might become an unnecessary casualty and should be replaced. Lewendon most emphatically thought otherwise, but the Brigadier agreed with the MO and Lieutenant Parrish took Lewendon's place in the team."

At 2200hrs the sleepers were aroused and a final search was made of all pockets and wallets for envelopes or other indications of unit identity. Few were found as everyone was very security conscious, but those that were discovered were duly burned.

Another hot meal was followed by a short but most impressive service conducted by the Battalion Padre, Captain G. Parry, CF, one of the most popular officers of the Battalion. He was killed a few hours later.

After the service the CO made a final address to the Battalion and at 2130 the column of vehicles moved off to the airfield. The column was a long one, as each aircraft had a lorry to itself to avoid any possibility of muddle.

Standing by

The mental attitude at this stage was interesting to note, there was no hysterically exaggerated high spirits, no wise-cracking from lorry to lorry, as was usual in an exercise. There was an atmosphere of quiet confidence not unmixed with, let us admit it, a certain amount of honest funk (fear).

The afternoon's preparations at the airfield reduced work to be done before take-off to a minimum. The time was spent mostly in smoking final cigarettes, drinking final cups of tea or putting camouflage paint on faces. This paint was carried in tubes like toothpaste and was about the same consistency, but dark brown in colour. It was found that, on drying out - which it did very quickly - it came off again in flakes, so most abandoned it and used soot off the bottom of the tea kettles instead.

Photo: Airborne Forces Museum

Blacking up

At 2330 the Battalion was airborne in thirty-three Stirlings. The final Met report suggested the possibility of a fairly strong wind over the DZ, but otherwise the weather conditions should be good.

Here Private Bill (Ernie) Elvin takes up the story: *"The Stirlings were large heavy planes. It was just like riding in a double decker bus, only nowhere so comfortable. To get out of the plane, we had to*

21

The Tale of Two Bridges

waddle to the rear and drop out of a hole shaped like a coffin. There was plenty of back-chat, they all had something to say, probably due to the excitement and nervous tension." Or, as Bob Tanner recalls: *"Normandy - scared? Not really, bloody petrified."*

The flight to the DZ took the Stirlings just over an hour and a quarter and Edgar (Eddy) Gurney describes the scene:

"I was a Sergeant of the 7th (LI) Battalion Parachute Regiment in the 6th Airborne Division, seated in the fuselage of a Stirling bomber. D-Day was a few minutes old. As we neared the French Coast, anti-aircraft shells started bursting all around the plane causing it to rock, but the pilot flew straight towards our target area near the village of Ranville. Suddenly, a red light appeared at the end of the aircraft, which denoted 20 seconds to the commencement of the drop. The tension could be cut with a knife; we were all as tight as bow-strings."

Private Elvin was sitting on the floor of the Stirling for his flight to France.

"If you told me I could not go, I would have cried my eyes out, as would any of my mates in the Platoon. You see we were all green, never having been in action before, we all wanted to have a go. We were all fully trained and honed to perfection. When we got near the dropping zone on France it was red light on, get ready to drop. The noise stopped - just men moving to the rear of the plane, the engines throttled back, then it was green light on - 'GO', and we were out and floating down over France."

'Stick' emplaning

Photo: Airborne Forces Museum

The Tale of Two Bridges

'Waiting to hook up' - during training

Photo: Airborne Forces Museum

Geoffrey Pine-Coffin with Tim Carew (left, military adviser) and Hollywood actor Alan Ladd during the making of the film 'The Red Beret'

Chapter Three

"Floating Down Over France"

The drop of the 6th Airborne Division was more scattered than planned. Although this helped to confuse the enemy as to the extent and the area of the drop, it also confused the 6th Airborne.

In the case of the 7th Bn many loads were dropped in the wrong places and some were not dropped at all, which meant that they were less than a third in strength, no wireless sets, machine guns, PIATs (projector infantry anti-tank) or mortars. The fact that men and machinery had gone astray was due more to there being a strong wind blowing in the area of the DZ than the occasional pilot error. One such incidence of pilot error resulted in two Stirling paratroop carriers from Fairford, one of which was carrying men of the 7th Bn, being shot down by German ack-ack fire and crashing near the village of Grangues. Forty-three soldiers, sailors and airmen died or were mortally wounded in these crashes. There were, however, eight survivors who were made prisoners of war. They were later shot by the Germans.

Bill Sykes found himself *"drifting across a moonlit road into an apple orchard"* with an eighteen-man rubber dinghy strapped to his leg. The reason for the dinghy? It was to ferry his group across the water if the bridges had been blown. He quickly realised that he was well behind enemy lines and, as he says, *"My major worries at that time were the two grenades that I was carrying and where was everyone else. The first thing I did, after disentangling myself from the nylon parachute, was to discard the dinghy - after seeing the devastating effects that grenades can have on a person. I was scared to death of the vague possibility that one of the pins, securing either of the grenades, may somehow get detached and cause my instant demise."*

THE TARGET AREA

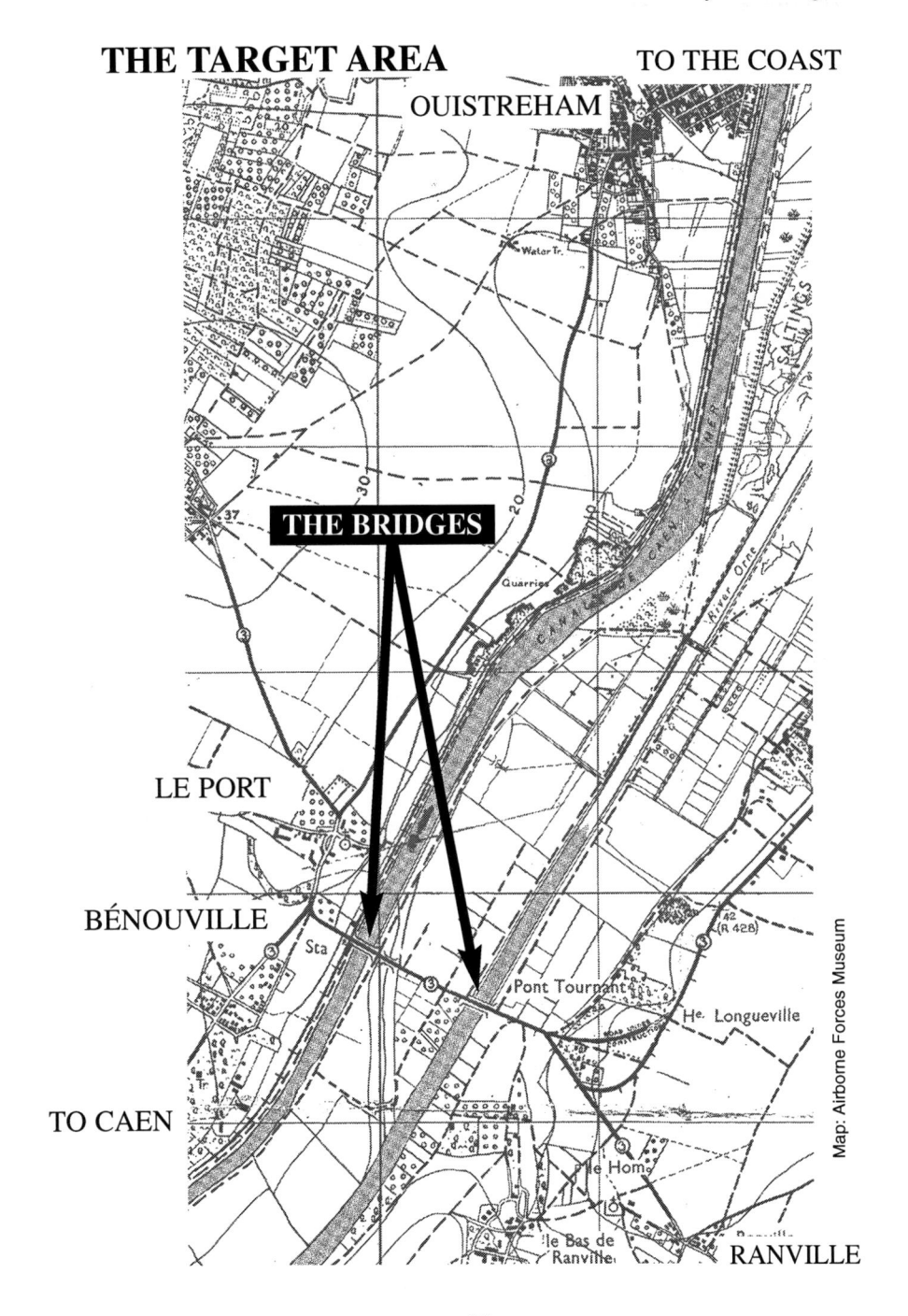

TO THE COAST

OUISTREHAM

THE BRIDGES

LE PORT

BÉNOUVILLE

TO CAEN

RANVILLE

The Tale of Two Bridges

    Others had also realised they were not on the DZ and were in wooded country on the upper slopes of a hill just above the village of Grangues, a short distance north east of the German Headquarters. They nearly ran into a large party of Germans, but narrowly missed detection by flattening themselves against the trees. Next they avoided a sentry and then ran into, and got themselves out of, a picketed mule train.

    Eddy Gurney had better luck, *"I was number 17, I stepped out into space, but just as I did so the plane rocked and I hit both sides of the hole during my exit, breaking my Army watch which I later found had stopped at 0036hrs. In the distance I saw a church which I instantly recognised as Ranville. I was in the right place at the right time. I heard a thump as my kit bag hit the ground, then I landed and for a full minute was violently sick. I can only think this was due to a sudden release of tension as I had never been air sick in my life."*

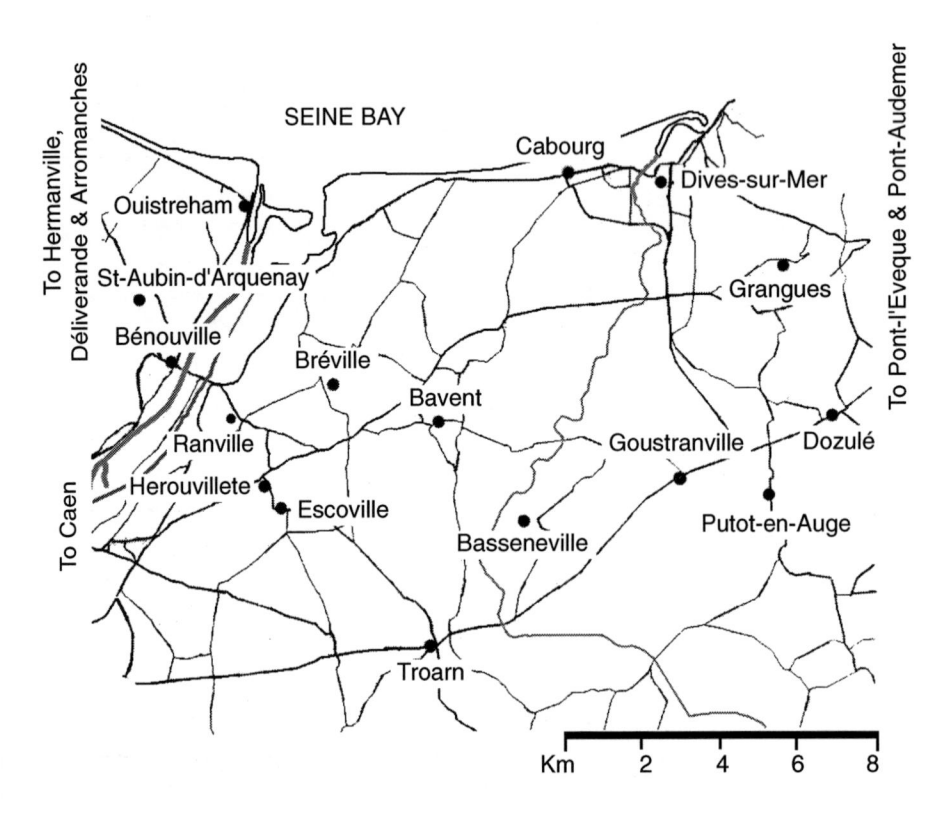

It had been found early on, that the wireless sets which had been put into a container were useless when they suffered the shock of hitting the ground and the container was also hard to find in the dark. The result was the Airborne Forces Development Centre devised a large, well padded kit bag which held as much as 100lb in weight of supplies. This was strapped to the parachutist's leg by the means of two quick-release straps. Into the kit bag was put the radios etc., attached to the bag was a long length of rope, the other end was fastened to the parachute harness. After leaving the aircraft the bag was lowered and hung about twenty feet or so below the jumper.

Bill Elvin who had been "floating down over France" takes up the story again. *"It was so silent, where was the war? Where were the Germans? Then I looked below, where was the land? Below me all was water as far as I could see. I panicked and set off the air levers on my Mae West-type jacket under my parachute harness (a big mistake). So there I was, like a real Michelin man being dragged over the water by my parachute, not being able to release myself from the harness, but luckily one of my section was close by and he waded over and cut me free so that I was able to stand waist deep in the water. We had landed in the flooded Dives Valley. The Germans had breached the banks of the River Dives, so flooding the ground as an anti-invasion obstacle and we were in fact miles from our objective."*

Bill Elvin encountered the Germans; he and five others had no idea where they were or where any of the others were as it was pitch black and silent. They got themselves out of the water, chose a direction and set off.

"We had not gone far down the road when an order was given in German. Two bursts of machine gun fire and grenades were directed at us and then silence. I dropped to the ground, flat as I could get, my heart thumping and thinking that after all the hard training I had been through, now I was going to be killed without even seeing a German. When we came to our senses there were only three of us left, where the other three went we did not know. Their bodies were not there, so they must have scattered in the confusion and not been killed."

Pine-Coffin (nick-named 'Wooden Box' by his men) noted: **"The pilots were having considerable difficulty pin-pointing the DZ,**

The Tale of Two Bridges

which was hardly surprising because the moon which should have been shining brightly was obscured at that time by clouds - as a result planes were running in from all angles, which greatly confused the men on the ground until they realised what was happening. The enemy had been caught by surprise, but soon made the DZ an unhealthy spot by firing across it from various positions. The Germans use tracer ammunition considerably and the sight of this criss-crossing over the ground presented a rather pretty picture to the descending parachutist from three hundred feet and, in some cases, considerably lower, so there was only about ten seconds in which to admire the display before it became much too personal for it to be appreciated. The advance party, who had jumped from the Albermarles thirty minutes before the main drop and included, as representatives from the Battalion, Lieutenant Rogers and Privates Wing, Moran, Starke and Styles, carried an Aldis lamp, with a green mask, as a rallying guide for the Battalion. Their Pilot had found it difficult to pinpoint the DZ accurately enough to drop them near any particular part of it and, as a result, Rogers, complete with his lamp, had not located the Rendezvous (RV) himself by the time of the main drop and was separated from the rest of his party."

He decided to flash the lamp, however, and so rally round his men of the Battalion, who could continue the search as a formed body. Curiously enough the first one to rally to him was the CO, who had landed on a road on which he bruised his heel which had slowed his progress.

One of the lighter incidents of the planning back in England centred round this Aldis lamp. When it was originally received, no batteries came with it and urgent signals were sent off for them. Instead of the batteries, however, a reply was received pointing out that this particular lamp was of a very modern and improved type and did not need any batteries as all you had to do to produce a beam of prodigious length was to plug it into the mains and switch it on!!

'Bill' Sykes, having landed safely without his grenades going off, now had to locate his partners, *"For recognition purposes we had been given a little tin gadget known as a 'Cricket' which when pressed emitted a clicking sound. The drill was to click once and receive a couple of clicks in return, or vice-versa. I clicked my cricket - nothing. I clicked again, nothing. One more try and the voice of the Platoon Sergeant (a man of few words, mostly four letter ones) boomed across the aisle between the apple trees, 'If that stupid little man who is doing that f...ing clicking, doesn't f...ing shut up, I'm going to f.....ing come over there and blow his f....ing head off,' so much for friendly fire!!"*

In the dark, noise and confusion of war, it was difficult for the men to pick out where they were. **"Myself and Lieutenant Rogers collected many wanderers in their search for the RV. It was a most desperate feeling to know that one was so close to it, but not knowing in which direction it lay. Time was slipping by and the coup-de-main party might well be in difficulties. Everything could so easily be lost if the Battalion did not arrive in time, it was impossible to pick up a landmark though until a chance flare, dropped by one of the aircraft, illuminated the church at Ranville, with its most distinctive double tower, and thus provided the necessary clue."**

The party arrived at the RV at 0145 and luckily included the CO's Bugler, Private Chambers, and of course the Aldis lamp.

The regimental call was sounded continuously in all directions and the light was flashed brightly, regardless of the unwelcome attentions they might attract. Officers and men began to come in from all sides and it was good to see how many had joined into groups to come in as formed bodies, with their own protective detachments, and the senior of the group in undisputed command, although there were several groups without either officers or NCOs.

The system that had been developed within the Battalion for reporting the state of forming up was for sub-units to pass to Battalion HQ, at regular intervals, their percentage strength. The figures were necessarily only guesses, but they enabled the CO to gauge when he was strong enough to move off.

The familiar messages soon started to come in, but they made depressing hearing: 20% was the first report from 'B' Company, 30% from 'A' Company and only 15% from 'C' Company.

The Tale of Two Bridges

The CO decided that time was more important than strength and elected to move off when three rifle companies reached 50% and leave his Second-in-Command, Major E. Steele-Baume, at the RV to bring in the remainder when he assumed that as many as could be expected had arrived.

Major Steele-Baume

'C' Company, although they were lightly equipped, was one of the weakest companies owing to several of their aircraft having dropped them wide of the DZ. Amongst those missing was Major Bartlett himself. Captain R. Keene (later promoted), the Company Second-in-Command, assumed command of the Company and was ordered to move off and carry out its mission at 0215hrs. He was then at approximately 40% strength.

The remaining two rifle companies, at just over 50% strength, with Advanced Battalion Headquarters, set off just behind them and at a slightly slower rate.

Major 'Tiger' Reid

7th L.I. Lost Again
by Tom Gould

The paras on the march again,
Mud and wind, sludge and rain,
Through Bulford, Amesbury,
Salisbury Plain,
Seventh Light Infantry, lost again!

On Pegasus Bridge we were about
But in the books they left us out
In the Ardennes through ice and snow
At each crossroads, "Which way to go?"
Was it Reid or was it Keene,
Who knew the way and where we'd been?

On the Rhine was just the same,
No-one seemed to know our name.
To India next, out on the plains,
To train with Fritz at jungle games.
Round and round we went each day,
"Lost again", we heard them say.

Singapore, Java, Siam too,
Some of the countries we went through.
In Palestine they changed our name,
Seventh Light Infantry, lost again!

Major Bob Keene

Chapter Four

Action

The 6th Airborne were now totally involved on all sides. The coup-de-main force had come in by gliders. The various Battalions were trying to regroup, deal with the enemy and proceed with all haste to carry out their orders, which were to seize and hold the bridges over the River Orne and Canal de Caen, then establish a bridgehead on the west bank of the canal until relieved by seaborne troops. The bridges were to be captured intact if possible, in addition a battery position, thought to be abandoned, was to be neutralised and occupied.

"This force (coup-de-main) landed as close to the bridges as possible at 0020hrs D-Day (6th June). This force consisted of a Company and two Platoons of the Oxfordshire and Buckinghamshire Light Infantry (with certain attached troops) under Major Howard (Ox and Bucks) and was carried in six gliders. Lieutenant McDonald travelled with this force for liaison duties between Howard and myself."

The coup-de-main party was successful and as a result it was not necessary for the Battalion to cross the water obstacles in dinghies as had been expected.

Eddy Gurney, who had earlier been violently sick on landing, was now one of a group of parachutists, and relates: *"One of the 20 to 30 parachutists was a wireless operator who was trying to contact the glider troops that had landed just before us near to the bridges and, we hoped, had captured them intact. We were about 200 yards from the first bridge when the wireless operator shouted 'Ham and Jam', the signal that the glider troops had captured the bridges intact. I immediately threw away my kit bag containing the dinghy that would have been used to cross the water obstacles had the bridges been demolished by the Germans."*

"The signals could now be heard plainly so the pace was stepped up, and soon the Orne bridge was reached and seen to be intact, with Howard's men on it. As the bridges were intact I took

Approximate positions of glider landings and drop zones

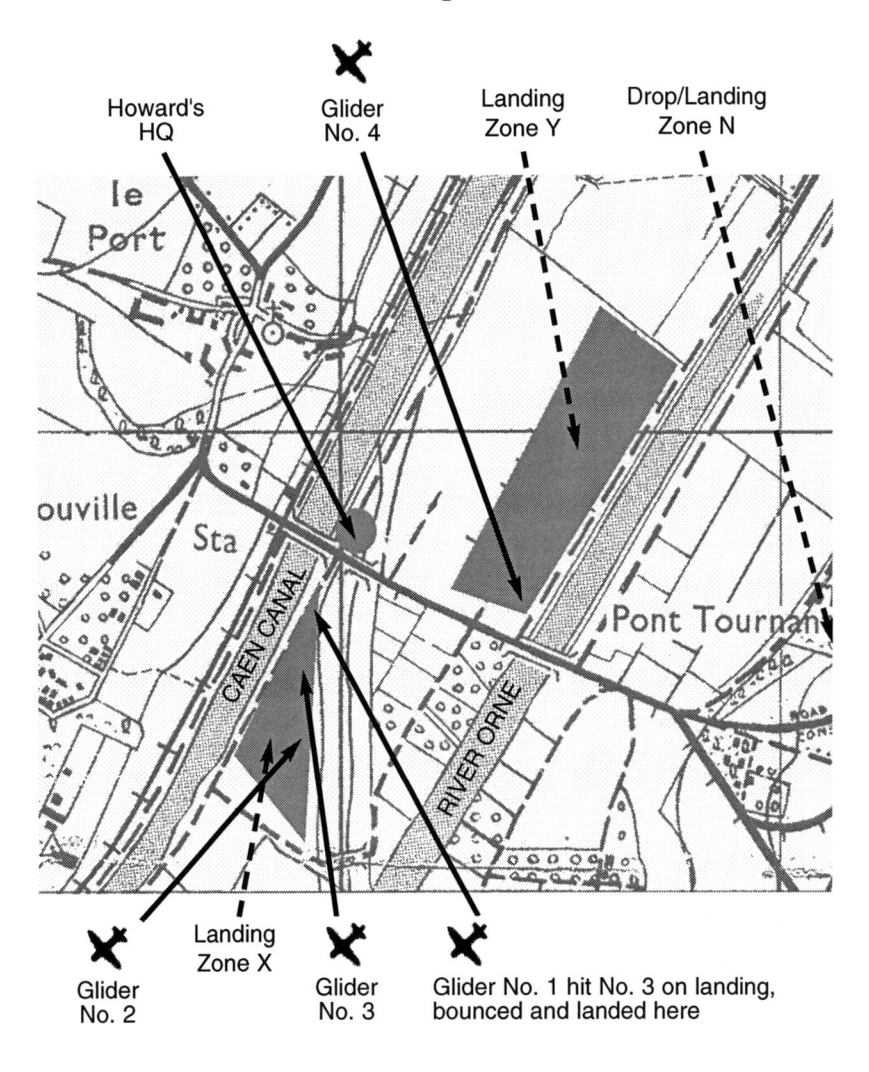

Howard's HQ · Glider No. 4 · Landing Zone Y · Drop/Landing Zone N

Landing Zone X · Glider No. 2 · Glider No. 3 · Glider No. 1 hit No. 3 on landing, bounced and landed here

✕ Glider No. 5 landed at Cabourg, on the coast to the east of Ouistreham

✕ Glider No. 6 landed nearer the coast, north of Ouistreham

my force over them with all speed and ordered them into their pre-arranged bridgehead positions in Bénouville. I had arranged in England with Howard to do this if he should be fighting on the west of the canal when I arrived; my positions were outside the area he was likely to be in with his small force and, by working around and into them, I would not only assist him but would also save time. It was 0140hrs when I crossed the canal bridge with this force."

Meanwhile, on the east side of the canal, Dennis Edwards, John Butler and an officer believed to have been Lt. Parrish, were having problems with an enemy gunboat.

John Butler writes, *"Just as we started to sally down the canal towpath towards the boat; there was a very loud bang from the opposite bank and a puff of debris from the superstructure of the boat, which went quickly into reverse and started to retreat back towards Caen. At the time I thought that the 'Glider Riders' had brought in a six-pounder anti-tank gun on the east side of the bridge.*

Not so. Fifty years later in correspondence with Dennis Edwards I found out that there had been a Jerry 37mm anti-tank gun on the east side of the bridge and that he and one Willy Parr and some others were trying to get the gun into operation when, as Dennis said, they must have pressed the right button, or pulled the right lever, for the gun fired. They had no idea that they had hit the target until I assured him these fifty years later. I had not only heard the bang, but had seen the strike."

"The occupation of the bridgehead positions called for some hasty decisions and reorganisation as no complete Platoon (or even section) existed as such. It was only possible to gauge the position of the companies by the sound of small firearms fire as there was no wireless. I contacted Howard and congratulated him on his success and was given a brief account on the situation.

Major J. Howard

Brigadier Poett, everyone was pleased to note, was also there and very happy looking he was too, as well he might be. Things were going well. Both bridges had been captured and both were intact. The simplest of plans could now be used and all the heavy boating equipment could be dumped.

When I judged that the positions had been occupied, at about 0210hrs, I ordered Howard (who came under my command at this stage) to withdraw his men over the canal bridge and made him responsible for the river bridge and the area between the two. The distance between the two bridges was only about four hundred yards, but it contained plenty of evidence of the thoroughness with which Howard's men had done their job.

Many of the Battalion got their first sight of a dead German on that bit of road and few will forget it in a hurry, particularly the one who had been hit with a tank-busting bomb whilst riding a bicycle. He was not a pretty sight. Steele-Baume and rear Battalion HQ, which still included no mortars, medium machine guns (MMGs) or wireless, joined me on the west bank of the canal at 0220hrs.

Howard's men were naturally in very high spirits and much friendly banter and chaff took place as the Battalion had hurried past them. They had done a most splendid job which rendered the task of the Battalion immeasurably easier. There would now be a bridgehead on the west side of the canal for certain and, with any luck at all, it would be as deep as planned too."

From about 0220hrs onwards the battle was very confused, fierce and almost continuous. The differing recollections reveal that it was almost impossible to get a crystal clear story of the fighting. However, the Brigadier had urged the Battalion to hurry and apparently the rest of the trip was done at the double by everyone. As Eddy Gurney explains: *"We raced onwards and as we approached the Caen Canal bridge, I saw a number of dead bodies lying in the roadway. On the other side of the bridge there appeared to be an almighty battle in progress, but this turned out to be ammunition exploding in a German tank that had been destroyed by the Glider Troops."*

The Tale of Two Bridges

"The leading troops crossed the canal bridge at 0240hrs and moved straight to their allotted positions. I took my stand by the canal bridge itself to deal with the various problems of the Commanders as they passed. The chief problems were connected with the various battle outposts, the loss of the wireless was particularly handicapping. 'B' Company were much troubled by snipers in Le Port and were also heavily attacked in their positions on the wooded escarpment. Soon after daylight the lack of mortars and MMGs became uncomfortably apparent and a modification of the original dispositions was called for."

Capt 'Waggers' Wagstaffe

The situation at first light was as follows: 'A' Company were fighting in their area, but runners failed to reach them, no runners came back from them and there was no wireless. The Company seemed to be surrounded because 'B' Company were, on occasions, attacked from the south, i.e. their ('B' Company's) left.

The regimental aid post (RAP) in 'A' Company's area had been over run and the Medical Officer, Wagstaffe of 225 Para Field Ambulance, was missing. The Padre, Lt. Parry, had been killed at the RAP. This was found out by the Intelligence Officer, Mills, who had gone to try and contact 'A' Company. The Battalion Medical Officer, Young, was also missing after the drop. He arrived by glider the next day together with his stick (usually 18 men) which had not been dropped. This stick also included the Officer Commanding HQ Company (Major Tullis).

Arnold Young, MO

"'B' Company were finding it difficult to retain their hold on the wooded escarpment and had only been able to dominate the southern half of Le Port. 'C' Company were almost completely split up into battle outposts. The battle outpost problem was a difficult one because each outpost was small and highly trained for its specific job. Now they were not complete. They had the best employment of specialists, such as mortar men, machine gunners and signallers, none of the containers had been recovered and they were, therefore, without their leader.

It had been intended to hold one Platoon of 'C' Company as a small reserve force at Battalion HQ, this was a small enough reserve in all conscience, but now it had to be reduced even further in order to bring the outposts up to strength. I had altered the original orders to these outposts about withdrawal but, as I could not communicate with them by wireless and did not consider runners reliable enough for such an important message, I ordered them to withdraw on their own initiative. Only under heavy pressure. None of them did so withdraw.

The outpost Commanders knew they had to remain in their areas whatever the opposition against them and, having given the Commanders the authority to withdraw, watched them move off into the night with considerable anxiety. These outposts did sterling work.

The rifle companies were about 50% strength (less casualties which they were suffering at the time). A few personnel of the mortar and MMG Platoons were available, but armed only with pistols. These I retained at my HQ to augment the counter-attack force which consisted of 'C' Company (less two Platoons and Commander (missing)).

These were all specially selected men and would be first class in action, but they were not now armed to fight at anything but close quarters. Each carried a pistol with which they would defend themselves if their specialist weapons were overrun, some had fortunately retained the Sten gun which every parachutist carries for immediate use on landing. Battalion HQ was established at 0230 in the position that had been selected for it from the model and it was then possible to reflect on the situation as it stood."

The Tale of Two Bridges

Eddy Gurney was part of 'A' Company and had crossed over the by-now captured bridges, turned left at a T-junction into the village at Bénouville:

"Slowly we crept through the village until we came to the large Iron Gates of 'The Chateau de Bénouville' which was situated on a minor cross-roads.

It was here that one of our party, Private McCara, climbed over a hedge and was (we believe) knifed to death by two Germans waiting on the other side. A number 36 hand grenade with a four seconds fuse was thrown over the hedge into the slit trench that the Germans had then occupied. We believe that the two Germans were themselves both killed by the grenade. A machine gun then opened fire from inside the Chateau gates wounding Private Whittingham (who later died of these wounds), and a German stick grenade exploded near the head of our officer who started to bleed from his eyes and ears, which gave us the impression that he had fractured the base of his skull, and so we withdrew, taking our wounded with us.

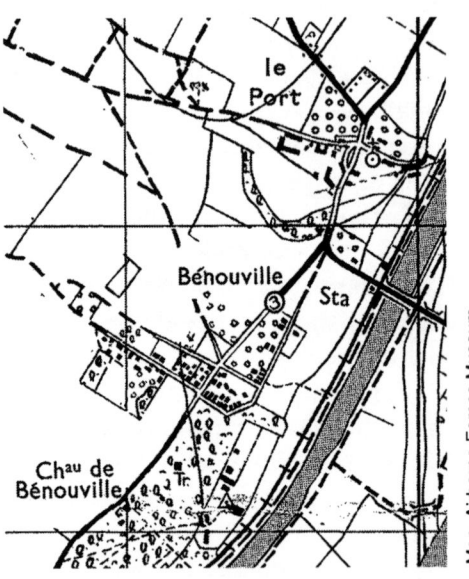

We set up a defensive position on a bank of earth bordering a sunken cart-track that was about ten feet wide. On the opposite side of the track and immediately in front of us was a seven foot wall with a wooden door at one end. We were now on the seaward side of Bénouville. Our position enabled us to control any enemy movement along the main Caen/Ouistreham road as well as preventing them from making any attack on the bridges from the western side of the village."

"I decided to hold the enemy on the line of the road running north-south from Le Port to Bénouville. The plan was for 'B'

Company to infest the southern half of Le Port and the wood on the north side of the road junction and to prevent any breakthrough to the bridge from the north. I held my counter attack force in the area of my HQ from which it could cover the small wood by fire and was well placed to launch a counter attack. The gallant fight being put up by 'A' Company I hoped would prevent any large-scale attack developing from the south. If it did so develop, however, the country was fairly open to the south of the bridge itself and I had placed one Platoon of 'B' Company (Thomas) in this position and felt confident that he could at least delay any attack from that direction for sufficient time for me to be able to take any necessary action. In a real emergency I would have brought a proportion of Howard's men back to the west side of the bridge, as the Battalion was now pitifully weak in numbers. The actual number available, in all ranks, did not quite touch two hundred, excluding Howard's party which could produce seventy more.

This plan worked well and during the course of the day's fighting the enemy launched eight separate attacks in addition to nagging constantly with small parties and occasionally armoured cars."

These skirmishes are reported by Eddy Gurney: *"The night was taken up by small skirmishes between German and our own patrols who were constantly probing to locate the enemy. At about 10.30am three large German tanks came rumbling along the main road from the direction of Caen. They stopped near the Chateau gates. Then the leading tank lowered its gun and fired a shell at the end of our position. Private McGee, who was near the main road, picked up his Bren gun then started to walk up the middle of the road towards the tanks, firing the Bren gun from his hip. As one magazine became empty, he replaced it with a new one, discarding the empty magazine on the roadside. We could hear the bullets ricocheting off the armour steel plating, the leading tank immediately closed down his visor thus making him blind to all things in front!*

Private McGee

Corporal Tommy Killeen realised what was happening and ran up the side of the road, taking two Gammon bombs from his pouches. He threw the first bomb which hit the leading tank where the turret meets the body, which nearly blew the turret off. He threw a second bomb but, being further away from the second tank, it fell short, landing against the tank's track, which was promptly blown off. This tank now tried to escape but, having only one good track, it went round in circles, so the crew baled out and tried to escape. They were shot by McGee.

Cpl Tommy Killeen

Next came an attack by about a Company of Panzer Grenadiers, but this was easily contained and they withdrew after losing a number of men.

I was now with Sergeant Young guarding the right flank when we saw a section of about 10 Germans break cover some 700 yards away on our western flank. We waited until they were on an open flat piece of ground, then opened fire with our rifles, which were fitted with telescopic sights. We didn't see any enemy movement on that flank for the rest of the day. It was just after this event when I saw L/Cpl Davey laying out in an orchard, his face covered with blood, and was just about to investigate when a German Panther tank appeared about 40 yards from our position, quite near to Davey. It stopped, lowered its large 88mm gun which now appeared to be pointing straight at me. I shouted a warning as I dived into a ditch, and the shell made a hole in the wall about 3 yards to my left, but we suffered no casualties. It was later learned that Davey had realised the Germans were all around him so he pretended to be dead. In fact he made his way to Pegasus bridge as soon as it was dark and was later returned to England with his wounds. After a period in hospital he rejoined the Regiment and survived the war.

During the many attacks made by the enemy that day (mainly by about a company strength) all were successfully dealt with at a considerable cost to the enemy, but our own casualties were now mounting. It was during one of these attacks that a German walked through the wooden door in the wall in front of us. He was just as surprised as us and immediately disappeared back through the door before we could react.

We had now been surrounded by the enemy since our arrival and so Sergeant Young and myself decided to try and get back to the canal bridge (Pegasus) to find out the position. As we travelled along the ditch, with Sergeant Young leading, a shot rang out and he shouted that they had broken his back. I pushed him down into the ditch and fell on top of him. Then I examined his wound which proved to be a furrow right across his back, but did not appear to have injured his spine. I gave him a morphine injection which we all carried and dressed his wounds before returning to our position."

These constant attacks are confirmed by Pine-Coffin. **"Excellent work was done here by the mortar officer (Archdale) who led numerous small patrols to break up parties attempting to come this way during the course of the day's fighting. I estimated that the organised attacks were delivered by about a company each time. The enemy showed little initiative and repeated the same attack time after time. Fortunately the dispositions suited the approach he chose. He usually attacked from the north west or west. Heavy casualties were inflicted on the enemy (many more would have been inflicted if I could have used mortars and MMGs) and all attacks were beaten off. No further closing in on the bridgehead was necessary.**

Lt Nick Archdale

The part of Le Port nearest to the canal was never completely cleared of snipers who made life a precarious affair in the area of Battalion Headquarters.

As soon as one was cleared from one place others would appear elsewhere, even to return to the same place. They were not very original although their courage could not be denied. The church tower was a particularly popular spot and was undoubtedly a first class choice, if rather an obvious one on the part of the sniper to use it. No sooner had one been silenced, usually with a large Bren gun, than another would start from the same place."

The Tale of Two Bridges

Finally the permission of the CO was sought to use a PIAT (projectile infantry anti-tank) on the tower itself. The permission was given and Corporal Thomas Killeen, with one bomb, blew the best part of the top of the tower clean off. Killeen was later interviewed by a BBC commentator on this interesting feat and, thinking that he had committed some dreadful offence by firing at the church at all, was at pains to point out that he had done as little damage as possible and had been most careful to remove his helmet when entering the church to see the effect. He had found the bodies of no less than twelve different snipers when he went up the tower.

Bénouville Church after Cpl Killeen's handiwork

Twenty of the tiny reserve held at Battalion HQ and consisting of part of a Platoon of 'C' Company and the mortar men and machine gunners were sent off with orders to break through the ring and report to Major Taylor as reinforcements. The mortar men and machine gunners, who were lightly armed with their pistols a few rifles and Sten guns, were to pick up rifles off the casualties that 'A' Company must inevitably have suffered. This party was commanded by Lt.

McDonald and duly achieved its objective. They remained with 'A' Company and provided a little, but welcome, relief. The fact that they had succeeded was not known at Battalion HQ, however, as the runner with the message was killed on his way back.

The German attacks were numerous and were pressed vigorously, but they made the mistake of under-estimating the strength of the Battalion and were attacking with forces of about a company strength only. The lack of mortars was sadly felt on these occasions, because there is no weapon more suited to dealing with an attacking enemy which has drawn back to reconsider its problem. Under such circumstances a few well-placed mortar bombs are likely to inflict more casualties than were sustained in the assault itself and may well prevent a further attempt altogether.

"...he had done as little damage as possible..."

Photo: Airborne Forces Museum

Chapter Five

The Battle Continues

'B' Company, under Major Neale, for its part was having plenty of excitement in covering the part of the village known as Le Port and blocking the approaches to the bridge from the west. Le Port included the block of houses comprising the village as well as the church. The chief approach from the west was a valley, which was covered by the wooded escarpment held by the Company, but used nevertheless almost continuously by parties of Germans trying to break through.

'B' Company was being attacked almost all the time by parties of varying sizes and saw a very great deal of fighting. This fighting developed more into separate Platoon engagements than a co-ordinated Company action which, although entirely effective, was somewhat disappointing for Major Neale. Lieutenant Farr's Platoon looked after the wooded escarpment while Lieutenant Poole and his Platoon were responsible for the houses in Le Port. Both, of course, had a totally different kind of fighting to carry out.

Lt Tommy Farr

The third Platoon, commanded by Lt. Thomas, was entrusted with the guarding of the vital canal bridge itself and was dispersed in a tight semi-circle round the west end of it. It was as depleted as any other Platoon and did its job with a small party, under Corporal Hutchinson, on the right. There was a similar party under Sergeant Fay on the left and Lt. Thomas himself with the remainder right by the bridge itself.

To quote the words of Lt. Thomas, *"The Platoon, having been deprived of the job of ferrying, and finding themselves reserve Platoon in the Battalion, had rather developed the idea that they had been left out of the show."*

In point of fact they were far from being the reserve Platoon. They were holding the divisional objective itself and it is doubtful if any other Platoon in the whole Division had such a responsible job as they did. Nevertheless No. 6 Platoon *"felt out of it"*.

The effects of inaccurate dropping can be seen very clearly simply by examining the case of this Platoon.

It had emplaned in two aircraft at Fairford: half of the Platoon under Thomas in one plane and the remainder under Sergeant Amey in the other. Thomas's stick was given an almost perfect drop and was put down square across the centre of the DZ so that the whole stick duly arrived at the RV and was later available at the bridge. The other stick was dropped some twelve miles from the DZ and it was several days before the bulk of the men managed to get back.

Each had several adventures on his way back and did very well to get through at all, but, in the meantime, the Platoon was compelled to do a complete job with only half its strength.

"One of the weapons which the Germans had installed for the defence of the bridge was a 40mm electrically fired gun. The Germans disrupted the wiring system before they left, but did no actual damage to the gun itself. Two of Thomas's men tinkered with it for a couple of hours and not only got it going again, but even zeroed it against a nearby bank. They found it fired 5 feet below at 300 yards. The gun was subsequently used, with great success, against snipers who fired from the windows of the chateau and at people crossing the bridge."

Bill Elvin was having his own problems. He still had no idea where he and his partners were. *"We carried on down the road and came to a farm just off the road with the buildings partly submerged. There was a faint light showing in a downstairs room, the occupants no doubt having been awakened by the firing. Now we had a chance to find out where we were!! So I knocked on the door while two others kept me covered with their weapons in case a German came to the door. Nobody answered, but a face appeared at the window. It was a man with a moustache and glasses. He shook his fist at us and made gestures for us to go away. We did not argue. We pretended to go away, but went round the other side of the farm and into a barn. The barn had a second floor, so we decided to go up there, rest and to have a view all round in case any Germans came down the road. We were*

The Tale of Two Bridges

all wet through and had to sort our equipment out. We came to the conclusion that if we waited until dawn, we would have a better chance of getting back to our Battalion in the daylight. We still had not got a clue as to where we were."

Back at the bridge the battle was still in progress and daylight had arrived, bringing with it a new set of problems.

"One of the chief problems of this bridge Platoon was how to deal with the very large numbers of extremely excited and voluble refugees who wanted to cross. They did not know which way they wanted to go, but were very frightened and wanted someone to take them under control. Obviously they could not be allowed to stream across whichever way they wished as there was always the chance that they would later contact the Germans and report what they had seen. There might even be Germans concealed among them. Thomas's Platoon had the job of separating the men from the women and children and herding them into hastily improvised cages. The obvious pleasure of these civilians at meeting British soldiers on the bridge was most noticeable and gratifying, but their attempts to shake hands personally with everyone had to be discouraged as it took so long.

The battle outpost in the grounds of the chateau reached its area, without difficulty, by 3am. It was commanded by Lieutenant Atkinson, who immediately put out a post to watch the road, which was the main one from Caen to the sea and the bridges.

Atkinson was an enthusiast for explosives and so were his men. Practically all of the party carried considerably more than their normal quota and the road party were particularly longing to use theirs on a tank. It is good to report that they were not disappointed and eventually destroyed one and crippled another which managed to keep moving but was later destroyed when it reached 'A' Company.

A systematic search of the chateau grounds was the next step and during this a mysterious figure was observed walking from the chateau itself towards one of the many outbuildings. A trap was laid and the figure walked right into it and was halted for interrogation. It was hard to tell if was a man or a woman, but it was certainly wearing trousers. It turned out to be Mme. Vian who was the matron of the maternity home which had its being in the chateau. Atkinson, who spoke fluent French, asked her for information and she gave him the location of every German in the grounds and added that there were two German doctors sheltering in the cellar of the chateau whom she found particularly unpleasant types. Mme. Vian had actually started the interrogation herself by asking who, and what, the soldiers were, which under the circumstances was a very reasonable question. She expressed great surprise and pleasure when she was told they were **L'ARMEE DE LIBERATION**, but more surprised and less pleased when she learned that their strength was one officer and nine other ranks!

When the interview was over, she asked if there was any objection to her going back to bed, whereupon she disappeared and presumably retired for the rest of the night!!"

The outpost soon established contact with various parties of Germans and, by reason of their position, undoubtedly helped to disorganise the attacks being staged against the Battalion from the Caen direction.

Their position also helped considerably to relieve some of the pressure on 'A' Company from the same direction. Just before the hour fixed for the start of the seaborne effort they heard a number of tanks forming up with the apparent intention of attacking the Battalion, but when the tank Commanders came forward on foot to receive their orders and get a view of their objective, they were able to inflict a heavy toll on them. Such an attack by tanks would have had very serious consequences as 'A' Company, which would have met it first, was in no condition to hold it for long and neither they nor the rest of the Battalion had the weapons to stop it completely.

However, the noise of the seaborne effort became very apparent before the Germans had recovered from the shock of being shot up. While on their feet the survivors rushed back to their tanks and the whole lot swung off towards the beaches.

The dawn has never been more welcome to anyone than it was to the Battalion on June 6th 1944. It is normally a dangerous time for troops in a defensive position and special precautions have to be taken, but as the attacks had been going on more or less continuously all through the night, it was improbable that there would be an effective dawn attack. There was nothing in particular to be done about it anyway as everyone was already on the alert. Soon after daylight all wearers of watches, and there are a great number in a parachute battalion, started glancing at them and comparing them with other people to see if they had lost or gained. All watches had been carefully synchronised before take off so everyone knew the exact second at which the Second Front would open up in earnest.

"**It was a curious feeling to be in such a privileged position and, at the same time, an extremely unpleasant one. The parachutist fights a rather lonely battle, forming an island in enemy country and defending it against attacks from any direction. They have no real front or rear and get the feeling that he is fighting a war all by himself. Now everyone knew the moment when all hell would break loose and when the enemy confronting him would be given something else to worry them, and what a worry too.**"

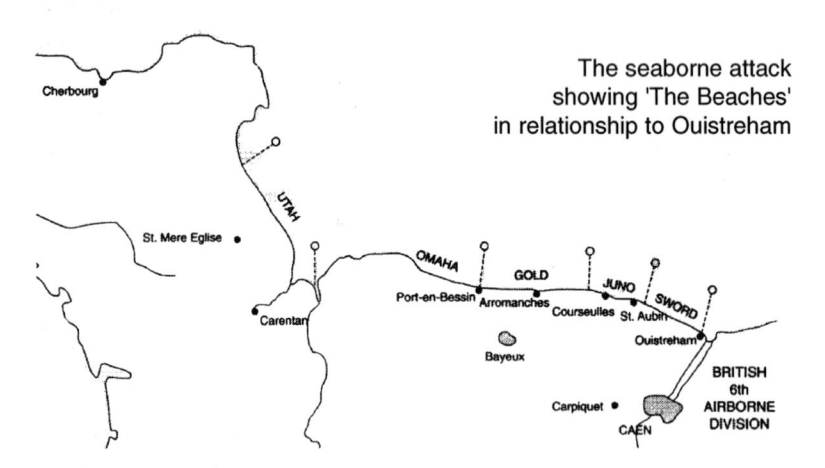

The seaborne attack showing 'The Beaches' in relationship to Ouistreham

By the time dawn arrived Bill Elvin and his party had dried out a little in the barn. *"So we made a move out of the farm and onto the road. In daylight we could see that each side of the road was flooded, but we made our way up the road and after going about a mile we could hear firing in the distance and so we knew that a battle was taking place. In time, we came to a driveway leading to a large house about 400 yards away. At the house we could see what appeared to be German soldiers on guard, so it was back into the water to make our way past, hoping we had not been seen. Nothing happened so we made our way back to the road. About 5 minutes later we came across a Frenchman and his wife coming down the road. The only thing we could understand was that there were no Germans the way we were going. So we carried on for a while and then saw men in the distance. We moved cautiously forward until we could recognise that they were Paras. When we got to them, it turned out that it was the 1st Canadian Para Battalion who were about to withdraw after using a bridge that they had blown up as a roadblock. So, into the water again we went and, holding onto the debris of the bridge, crossed to the other side and withdrew with the Canadians.*

As we withdrew, we saw signs of a battle. Paras were hanging from the high tension cables strung from pylon to pylon, their chutes caught in the cables from which they could not free themselves and that was where they met their deaths.

We withdrew with the Canadians all that day, those in front clearing away any German opposition. (It was only light opposition, the Germans not having recovered from the shock of our airborne landing. This was only D-Day and no doubt they would soon recover.)

Late that evening we ended up at the 3rd Para Brigade HQ at Lemesnil [at last he knew where he was]. *It was a very noisy night, so by midnight on D-Day, although I knew where I was, I had still not joined up with my Battalion."*

The men were still glancing at their watches:

"There were some very wry faces when the watches pointed to 7am and nothing could be heard except the small arms firing and bursting of mortar bombs which everyone had got used to. We had overlooked the fact that H hour, 7 am, was the time at which the guns would be fired and not the moment when we would hear the explosion of the shells. Actually the ships were some distance out in the Channel and the shells took a measurable time themselves to reach their targets and the sound of the explosions took further time to travel the three odd miles to battle position. It was a full minute after seven when the sound was heard.

The Tale of Two Bridges

"The noise, when it came, far exceeded all expectations and was quite indescribable both in intensity and duration, but it was music to the Battalion and spirits rose with the rumbling of it. The sense of fighting a lone battle passed completely, even fatigue was forgotten. The big show had begun and now it would only be a matter of time before the seaborne troops arrived on the scene and the battle for the bridge could be regarded as completely won."

The attacks on the Battalion bridgehead continued to be launched and to be beaten off, more as a matter of routine than as part of a life and death struggle on which everything depended. It seemed impossible that they could break through now and confidence was higher than at any period since the drop. The enemy was very persistent though and although the attacks were beaten off they were not without casualties. Each attack cost a few more men and those who were still unwounded were beginning to feel the strain.

Snipers elsewhere continued to be troublesome, too, and the anti-tank Platoon Commander, Lt. Archdale, whose Platoon was distributed round the Companies in detachments (Killeen had the one with 'B' Company), led at least ten separate raiding parties into the village area during the day. It was largely due to his efforts that the sniper problem did not develop into anything more serious than a nuisance.

The first seaborne troops to be expected were the 1st Commando Brigade under Brigadier The Lord Lovat, DSO, MC, who were to pass over the bridges into the divisional area and there come under command. They had vowed to cross the bridges by noon and from 11am onwards ears were strained for the sound of their bagpipes, which was the pre-arranged signal to be answered by the bugle if the way to the bridges was clear. True to their word the Commandos were first to arrive, but it was not until 1pm that their pipes could be heard in the distance.

"The temptation to reply by bugle was strong but had to be resisted because the way was not clear. Attacks were still being launched on the Battalion position and there was also snipers in

Le Port, and until the whole of Le Port was cleared this was not the case.

Private Chambers was forbidden to sound off and the Commandos made a slower and more cautious entry into Le Port than they otherwise would have done."

They came through in grand style and their mere numbers were sufficient to keep the snipers quiet for an hour or so. (After the Brigade passed through Le Port the snipers returned to the northern part from which they were never completely cleared.) There was much mutual interest in the meeting because, although Paratroopers and Commandos have much in common, they had not worked together before.

"There was plenty of time for chatting anyhow as the actual crossing of the canal bridge was to be something of a ceremony which took quite a bit of organising. Eventually it was all teed up and at 2pm the piper led the way across the bridge, skirling away on his pipes, followed by Lord Lovat. It was an impressive sight and they got across without a shot being fired at them."

Later parties were not so fortunate and a few casualties were suffered from snipers who opened up from the upper windows of the chateau onto the bridge. It was during this phase that Thomas's two amateur gun repairers did good work with their electrically-controlled gun.

A curious period of many hours followed the passage of the Commandos through this position. They had rushed through at remarkable speed well ahead of the remainder of the seaborne troops, clearing a narrow corridor for themselves as they went. Their passage had opened up the main road from the beaches temporarily, but had no effect on the Germans on the Caen side or even those off the road to the immediate west. During this period there were several more sharp battles and further casualties were inflicted and suffered.

The seaborne Battalion with which contact was to be made and which was to relieve the Battalion of the defence of the bridges, did not turn up. Instead various other small seaborne elements did appear, having profited by the opening of the road by the Commandos. These were somewhat at a loss to know what to do as they were well ahead of the infantry and were, for the most part, not fighting troops themselves. They were mostly lorry drivers and technical troops. They were of great interest to the men of 'B' Company in whose area they halted as they could give a first hand account as to how the beach landings had gone.

"**More interesting still they carried a liberal supply of the most excellent soups and drinks in patent self heating tins which were carried by the seaborne troops. They were not carried by the airborne troops as they could, of course, be used only once and were not an economical load. The lorry drivers seemed to have collected a few extra ones and these were handed out generously to those that were near to them. These were particularly welcome as few had had the chance to brew up a hot drink and kept going on biscuits and chocolates."**

One of the first to arrive was an elderly soldier driving a bulldozer by himself as his first mate had been killed during the landing.

"**He was a great character, very proud of the fact that he came from Yorkshire and whose chief worry in life seemed to be that he had been allotted a less powerful bulldozer than some of the other drivers in his unit although he was senior and, in his opinion, much the best one. He thought that life was very unfair and full of hardships."**

All through the day the efforts to reach 'A' Company had been going on and at one time a large part of the valuable reserve provided by the coup-de-main party was brought over the bridge into the area of the Battalion Headquarters in order to relieve every available man. These were formed into a force and sent off under the command of Lt. Archdale to get through to the Company. They succeeded in doing so and did invaluable work in bringing out casualties. They found the Company was very scattered and the job of contacting them was far from easy because of this. Soon after this party had started out Captain Webber, Second-in-Command of 'A' Company, got himself back to Battalion Headquarters and gave a verbal report. He had been wounded himself, but nevertheless made the journey. He reported that Major Taylor had been wounded and that all the officers were casualties. Control was difficult, but the position was still in the hands of the Company and morale was high, although the men were now getting very tired. Webber should have been evacuated himself (he was later found to have had a bullet through the lung), but as he was the only officer who really knew the situation there and, what was more important, the only person who could find his way back, he was allowed to carry on and make the return trip. He was to contact Lt. Archdale on his way back and make what use of that force he wished.

"At 7pm General Gale paid another trip to the Battalion and informed me that he was then in touch with the seaborne troops by wireless and that he had informed them that the relief of the Battalion must be treated as a first priority job. He gave generous praise to the efforts of the Battalion and chatted with the casualties who were in the first aid post at the time.

'A' Company were, as suspected, surrounded and hard pressed, but nevertheless fighting back hard. A counter attack was clearly necessary to enable them to collect in their wounded and re-group. I detailed the Platoon of 'C' Company who formed my counter attack force (Lt. McDonald) for the job and replaced them temporarily with a Platoon from Howard. Webber led this Platoon to 'A' Company area which involved working their way through the attacking Germans. The Platoon was, however, not strong enough (only about 17) to launch an attack that had sufficient effect on the attackers and in the end reinforced 'A' Company was itself surrounded. Its presence brought little relief to the Company however. 'A' Company had been fighting for 17 hours, unassisted, against superior numbers of infantry supported by tanks and self propelled guns. 'A' Company destroyed one Mark IV tank and one self-propelled gun with Gammon bombs. The Company was in good heart, but tired and weakened by casualties.

The position at this stage was not very comforting because, although I felt confident of holding off attacks for some time to come, there still seemed no prospect of relief for the Battalion and I could not be certain how things would go during the night, especially if the enemy decided to make a really determined attack with a large force."

The Tale of Two Bridges

The GOC, Major General Gale, sent out a special Intelligence Officer to explain the situation and to urge relief for the Battalion. GOC 3rd Infantry Division, immediately visited the area himself and ordered the 2nd Warwicks to take over. It was understood that the 3rd Infantry Division had been under the impression that the bridges had been re-captured by the Germans and that a large-scale attack by them (the 3rd) would be necessary to get them back. This attack was to be put in the following morning. The East Yorks had had very heavy casualties on the beaches and were unable to reach St. Aubin, much less relieve the Battalion at Bénouville.

The Warwicks came up very quickly (arrived at 2115hrs), but the take over involved an attack to relieve 'A' Company and evacuate their casualties. The Battalion finally crossed over the bridge (canal) at 0100hrs on D-Day plus one after handing over its positions to the 2nd Royal Warwicks. The bridgehead had been held by the Battalion for 21 hours.

'Pegasus' Bridge - The first casualties being evacuated

Photo: Airborne Forces Museum

The same day Bill Elvin, along with others, was on the move again. *"D-Day plus one, in the morning we were loaded onto a jeep to take a very hairy journey to 5 Para Brigade HQ. The two Brigades had not yet joined up, there were still German positions in between the two. I got back to 4 Platoon 'B' Company 7 Battalion at about 11.30am. They were dug in opposite Ranville church. In the distance I could see wrecked gliders and the Germans beginning to infiltrate them. We were being shelled spasmodically. I shared a trench with Private Bushell who told me what had happened. On the west side of the bridges over the Orne and the Canal, several men were missing from the Platoon.*

I was back where I should have been after taking a roundabout route. I felt safe to be with my old mates. Little did I know that by D plus 12 it would be a very small Platoon, with the Company Commander and Platoon officers wounded, the Company Sergeant Major killed, many NCOs I had trained with gone, killed, wounded, missing. The Company bled to white to hold the Germans back from re-taking the bridges and pushing the bridgehead back into the sea."

The numbers that Bill Elvin refers to were estimated as follows:

"Killed 18 - including 3 officers, Parry, Bowyer, Hill. Wounded 36" signed by Pine-Coffin in the field.

The Battalion was to spend the night in the village of Ranville close to the DZ where they had dropped some sixteen hours before. As sub units were relieved they were to move straight back to Ranville without waiting for further orders.

"I stationed myself on the bridge itself again to check them over. Bit by bit they came through. Tired, dirty, hungry and many of them wounded as well, but all marching with their heads held high. In amongst them were troops of the Air Landing Brigade who had come in during the late afternoon in what seemed a never ending stream of tugs and gliders to land on both sides of the two water obstacles. These formed an odd contrast with their freshness and cleanliness, to the battle weary men of the Battalion."

Brigadier Poett frequently visited the bridge at this period to chat to the men as they passed and to praise them for the job they had done. The men, for their part, remembered how he had also visited them in the afternoon before the take off while many of them slept. And how he had jumped with the pathfinder party thirty minutes before them. How his duties had kept him on the move from unit to unit ever since. **"He must be as tired as they were, probably more so. Indeed he looked tired too, but now he spoke only of their fatigue and of their good work so that a casual observer might have thought that he had done nothing himself."** He was a great leader and this was perhaps realised for the first time by many as they passed over the bridge.

Brigadier Poett frequently visited to chat to the men

**"By 9.30pm myself and Lt. Mills (IO) had a period of complete inactivity in front of us for an indefinite period. The Battalion was all across the bridge except for 'A' Company and ourselves; the relief of 'A' Company was taking longer than expected. The responsibility for the defence of the bridge had already passed to

The Tale of Two Bridges

the relieving Battalion and there was nothing to do but wait for the relief to be completed. The difficulty was to keep awake and this could best be done by constant movement, so myself and Mills moved up and down watching anything of interest that we could find.

Time passed slowly and it was gathered from reports coming in that the Germans were proving very difficult to dislodge from some of the houses in 'A' Company's area.

Lieutenant Mills

They were using their usual tactics of shooting from one house and then moving to another so that the attacking troops would enter an empty house and very often come under fire as they did so from another direction. The Company were working their way through the village systematically and every now and then small parties of 'A' Company would come back as they were relieved.

It was impossible to keep anything like an accurate check on the casualties as some were being evacuated towards the beaches direct through the seaborne field ambulances, whereas those handled by airborne field ambulances were evacuated over the bridges into Ranville. It was well after midnight when the last of the troops of 'A' Company came through the bridge and, after a final check up, myself and Mills passed over the bridge ourselves, this was just after 1am.

Thus ended the first day of action for the Battalion. It had been a particularly full day and had cost much blood and sweat, but the objective had been achieved and it was a comforting thought to reflect that, during the whole 23 hours of operation, not a single German other than prisoners had set foot on the bridge.

With the arrival of the seaborne forces the west side of the divisional bridgehead was secured firmly and the whole Battalion was freed to face the other way and re-join the rest of the Division."

Chapter Six

The Divisional Bridgehead

After its exertions of D-Day the Battalion spent what was left of the night in a large field just outside the village of Ranville. All ranks were dog tired and it was difficult to resist the temptation to lie down at once and sleep.

This temptation had to be resisted though and, after an all-round defensive position had been sighted, the next hour or two was spent digging slit trenches.

"**The trenches dug that night were a travesty of the text book examples as practically everyone, when they dug down about a foot, fell into the trench and was asleep immediately.**

Sentries were changed every half an hour as a precaution against falling asleep. This was not too severe a strain as there were only four more hours before daylight and it was interesting to note how extremely accurate the briefing models had been in comparison to the real thing, and to try to spot where one's wanderings after the drop had taken one. The whole area was now covered with gliders and bits of these were found to be very useful for making head covers for the slit trenches. There were few who were not experts at digging slit trenches by this time, but these became very quickly as good as the rest as it was frequently under accurate shell and mortar fire from across the DZ. Several casualties were suffered as a result of it because it is not possible for everyone to live, like a mole, permanently below the level of the ground. It is, in fact, an extremely bad thing if anyone develops a tendency to do so. Life continued more or less normally despite the shelling and everyone became very quick at diving into cover."

The seaborne elements of the Battalion, which included the bulk of the drivers and various administrative personnel, rejoined in this position and were quickly discouraged from swapping experiences with their friends and were employed on digging slit trenches for themselves. Whilst they were engaged in this task the area was

The Tale of Two Bridges

DZ 'N' - Breville top left - Road to Ranville and Le Mesnil (cleared by 7 Para) bottom left to right

shelled and an unlucky one fell right amongst them. Inexperienced as they were at that time, they heard it coming and dived for their trenches, but few had got in deep enough to get proper protection. More casualties were suffered, including a Private who was also the Battalion butcher and who was unfortunately killed.

The Germans seemed very slow to react and contented themselves with this shelling and mortaring from a comparatively long range and with the slipping of small parties of men onto the DZ to snipe from the many gliders lying there.

"This resulted in some amusing incidents occurring in this connection because the gliders were an object of interest to both sides and nothing will prevent a British soldier from looking at things that are a novelty to him. Parties of two or three would slip

out of their position onto the DZ itself with the object of exploring the nearest glider, but from this one they would pass onto the next and so on until they got well out onto the DZ. Several such parties bumped into similar German parties who had, presumably, left their own lines for the explorations of the gliders too. Often the Germans would surrender, but sometimes they would make a fight of it. It was an unnecessary risk for men to take but, fortunately, no harm came of it and the Wehrmacht was deprived of a few of its men as a result.

Commandos were at somewhat of a loss when a couple of men, who had not permission to be out at all, returned to their area, proudly escorting a party of prisoners or bringing in documents of Germans, who had decided to fight it out but had lost the fight."

It seemed that the Germans were, at last, about to make a serious attempt to recover the DZ, as considerable numbers of them could be seen moving into the area from the woods to the east of it. The MMG Platoon were the first to spot them, but the mortars were not far behind. Neither were Privates O'Sullivan and Woolcott, who were both crack shot snipers.

The MMG and mortar Platoons were under the command of Lieutenant Archdale at this time, following the death on D-Day of both the Battalion's machine gun officers (Lt. Bowler, the Brigade's machine gun officer, and Lt. Hill, the Battalion one).

"When I arrived on the scene, this was in response to a request to open up 'on large numbers of the enemy located in the open', I found that the snipers could fire immediately as they had all preparations in anticipation. I gave the word."

The range was just about a mile, but this was very suitable for MMGs and mortars and they took a heavy toll. O'Sullivan and Woolcott had a real field day too. It was particularly pleasing that the mortars and MMGs got this opportunity to target because theirs is one of the most thankless of all parachutists roles. Their weapons are heavy and complicated, calling for considerable skill to operate, and great physical strength and endurance to carry. Their own weight limits the amount of ammunition that is available, as both ammunition and weapon have to be carried on the back.

It is a point of honour that both Platoons keep up with the rest of the Battalion, wherever they go and at whatever speed. The men are picked for their size and strength, but they show a deal of initiative as well and it is no uncommon sight to find wheelbarrows or even prams being used for their loads when the going is suitable.

Parachutists are not tied to the roads though and more often than not move across country, which means a long and tiring carry for these specialists. They may hump their weapons and ammunition for days on end without ever being called upon to fire them. An opportunity to target from a static position, where extra munition has been dumped, is like manna from heaven to them and, like the Israelites before them, they made the most of their opportunity.

"**The attack was halted and the attackers, being badly shot up, made for the nearest cover, which was a series of small woods which lay immediately between the two parachute Brigades, but were not occupied by either. Their presence there was highly undesirable as they were, literally, a thorn in the side of both Brigades; a thorn in a very awkward side too, being just beyond the comfortable reach of either Brigade.**"

The Battalion was ordered to clear the woods and then to move on and establish contact with 3 Brigade. The operation was to take place that afternoon, when a squadron of tanks would be available for support. The Battalion had not co-operated with tanks before, so this would be an interesting little operation.

"**It was not expected that there would be any difficulty in carrying out the job, as the enemy must be considerably disorganised and would be numerically inferior, without food, reserves of ammunition and altogether in pretty poor shape. A bullet travels just as fast though, whatever the odds against the first man who fires it, and in this attack, as in any other, men of the Battalion would be killed and others wounded. It was altogether a thoroughly unpleasant job, generally considered 'a bit of cake', with little kudos for success and much blame for failure. It was nevertheless a job and an important one too.**"

The woods in question, known as the Le Mariquet woods, were three in number and rectangular in shape. From the map and air photos they

The Tale of Two Bridges

looked like three dominoes that had been placed originally end to end, but the end one had later been shifted out of line so that it now contacted its neighbour at one corner only. This displaced one was thicker than the other two and probably contained the bulk of the Germans.

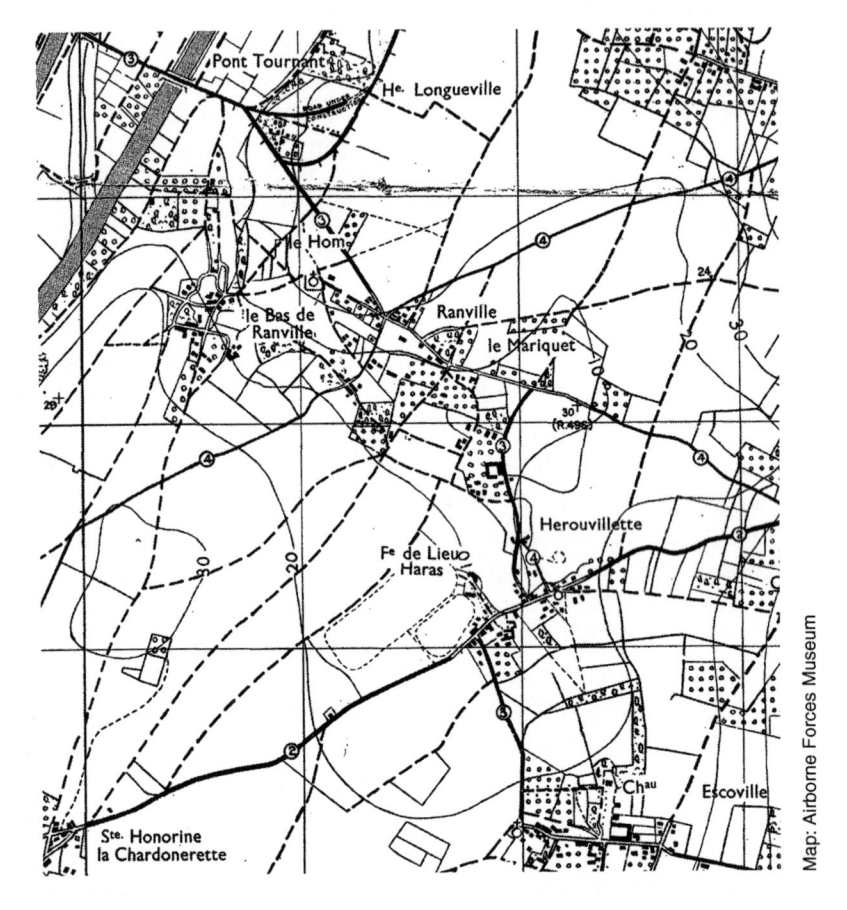

"It was difficult to determine the nature of the country beyond the woods, it looked like grass, probably was, but might be anything and of any height. Two features were quite definite though, first a road which bordered the long side of the displaced wood, to continue into 3 Brigade area, and second a track which branched off from this road at right angles, to cross the end of the displaced wood at a distance from it of 200 yards.

Control would be difficult in the woods, particularly against an enemy in scattered positions and employing sniper tactics, which was more than probable.

An extremely simple plan was laid on, which would allow for plenty of modification as the situation developed."

Briefly the plan was as follows: the tanks, the Commander of which had still to be consulted, were to advance first and lie off each wood, in turn firing into them for exactly two minutes with everything they had. When they finished at one wood they were to fire a smoke shell as a signal to the Battalion then move onto the next wood. After they had dealt with the third and last wood, the displaced one, they were to return to their base and the Battalion would finish the operation without them.

Only two rifle companies were available as 'C' Company had been employed, on the Brigade Commander's orders, to fill a gap in the divisional bridgehead in that part of the village of Ranville known as Le Bas de Ranville. They could not be released.

'B' Company and Advanced Battalion HQ would clear the first wood and 'A' Company and Rear Battalion HQ would then pass through them and clear the second. Whilst 'A' were clearing this second one 'B' would shift across in preparation to tackle the displaced one. When given the word to go they would move straight through it and continue until they reached the track running across its front. At this stage it would be necessary to issue further orders.

'A' Company at this period was completely denuded of its original officers as they had all become casualties during the struggle on D-Day. The officer casualty rate had been higher than that of the other ranks throughout the Battalion, but in this particular Company it had been the full 100%.

Lieutenant Parrish was appointed to command and this was to be his first action as Company Commander.

The tanks proved to be a squadron of 13/18 Royal Hussars (Shermans) and the meeting between Pine-Coffin and the squadron Commander, Major Rugge Price, who was accompanied by his own CO, took place at the

Lt Parrish

spot on the edge of the DZ which had been the Battalion's RV after the drop. They met at 1.30pm. The weather was, of course, playing its part.

"It was raining hard at the time and conditions for reconnaissance were further complicated by the presence of an unusually large number of Germans in the gliders on the DZ. These were being kept under close observation by the troops in the vicinity, who were having quite a serious shooting match with them and did not appreciate the sudden appearance of various officers, complete with binoculars and a desire to study their battlefield. It is only fair that the officers were none too keen either, but they could not do their job from anywhere else. The plan was eventually agreed to and the tank Commander decided to do his approach and firing from the DZ side of the woods."

The operation was to start at 4pm. The troops moved off to their start point, which was at the extremity of 13th Battalion's area, with 'B' Company and Advanced Battalion HQ leading and all were ready and in position to start by 3.40pm.

The twenty minutes' wait was spent chatting with the troops of the 13th Battalion, during which a deal of good-natured leg-pulling took place on the subject of having to call in the 7th to make things safer for the 13th. One of the most striking characteristics of the parachute troops was this feeling of great friendliness between the different units, which enabled them to give and take without any ill feelings on either side.

"The 13th Battalion accepted the jibe and retaliated by pointing out that the job was such an easy one that it had been considered safe to leave it to the 7th."

Punctually the tanks rumbled into view and with them the first problem arose. There were only two of them, but others could be heard following; they were moving slowly and it was obvious that not more than the leading two would be in position at the right time. Would the next two come up and fire their two minutes' worth on arrival regardless of the time, or would they pass by without firing to engage the second target?

The CO decided to hold 'B' Company until he was quite certain that the tanks had finished firing, even if this meant delaying the start until after the prearranged time.

The Tale of Two Bridges

"It soon became obvious that only eight tanks were going to appear and that those were employing tactics which were not strictly in accordance with the plan. The first two laid off from the first wood and fired into it exactly as planned, but the others went straight past and fired into the other woods as soon as they arrived, which was, of course, well before the infantry could get there. As a result the Germans were completely shot up and many of them killed, but the tanks remained stationary for anything up to twenty minutes and paid the penalty for doing so. Five out of the eight were hit by anti-tanks guns and went up in flames. Fortunately the crews escaped in each case, but from a taxpayers point of view it was an extremely expensive operation.

'B' Company led off a few minutes after 4pm, followed by Advanced Battalion HQ, and found that the first wood was no more than an orchard and the second one not much thicker. They were ordered to take them both while 'A' Company were moved onto the start line to tackle the displaced wood.

'B' Company found nothing in the orchard, but encountered a bit of trouble from snipers in the thick hedges bordering the second wood.

Major Neale, the Commander, very wisely ignored the snipers until he had reached, and secured, the limit of his objective. He could then afford to locate and deal with them one by one. He went after one of them himself, together with Private Cornell, his runner."

Cornell was to distinguish himself greatly throughout the campaign, earning the DCM and promotion to Sergeant in the process, only to be killed in the final battle which took place just ten months later, on the bridge at Neustadt.

Private 'Darkie' Cornell

Neale and Cornell were engaged in a game of cat and mouse. "**The two worked themselves back inside the hedge until they got a view of the sniper, whom they promptly shot, but not before he got a**

The Tale of Two Bridges

lucky shot himself which hit Major Neale in the leg. The wound was a serious one which necessitated Neale's evacuation at the time and was, later, to cause him the disappointment of being barred by a Medical Board from leading his Company on further operations.

The evacuation of Neale presented a problem of command as Captain Braithwaite, the Second-in-Command, had already been evacuated himself following injuries received in the initial drop. Captain Keene was later moved across from 'C' Company and assumed command of 'B' Company and promoted to Major."

'B' Company killed, and captured, some 40 Germans in their woods and then covered the advance of 'A' Company by firing into the displaced woods from the flank.

'A' Company's wood was very thick with heavy undergrowth and they were lost to view as soon as they entered it, so that their progress could only be followed by the sounds of firing and the occasional shouts and screams that arose. This little action was one of the few occasions when the Battalion used their bayonets and it was this that produced the screams.

This displaced wood was divided laterally and could really be regarded as two woods instead of one; Pine-Coffin was prepared to pass 'B' Company through 'A' on this dividing line if necessary. It turned out to be not only unnecessary but impossible because the Company streamed over the dividing line and didn't stop until they reached the far end of the second wood.

It had not been possible to see them across the division because of the undergrowth so Pine-Coffin with 'B' Company was uncertain, for a time, whether the second half had been combed or not. To make quite certain he pushed 'B' Company through it as well.

He need not have worried because when the end was reached, there was 'A' Company securely in position with a party of 60 or more prisoners.

"These prisoners presented a curious spectacle, as the Second-in-Command of the Battalion, Major Steele-Baume, who had been leading Rear Battalion HQ, had taken personal charge of the disarming and searching of them and was having it carried out with the utmost thoroughness. They were formed up in three ranks, suitably spaced out, and had laid all the contents of their pockets and pouches on the ground in front of them, as if for a kit inspection. When Advanced Battalion HQ arrived on the scene, they had just been ordered to remove their jackets as well and were all standing rigidly to attention and looking very silly indeed in their vests.

They were a much older lot than one would have expected and many of them had grey hair and lined faces. They all seemed very glad to be out of the war with a whole skin.

The collection of prisoners and their despatch to the rear took rather a long time so I decided to take a risk over the remainder of the drive in order to complete the whole operation without further delay. 'B' Company were passed through 'A' onto the track, with orders to push right on, keeping direction by the road on their right flank. Advanced Battalion HQ would follow them up and would move along the road itself".

This risk was fully justified because the final stages turned out to be an anti-climax. There was no further opposition, but instead a Captain of the 3rd Brigade was waiting, with some impatience, at the objective. This Captain conducted Pine-Coffin to his Brigade HQ, which was in a large house some half a mile up the road. While they were on the way, however, Brigadier Poett, who was never far behind the leading troops, came up the newly-opened road in his jeep and their whole party continued the journey on wheels.

This meeting of the two Brigadiers was a great event, but no time was wasted on dramatics. Each told the other of locations of his own troops and the plan for the link up was reached. The Battalion was to remain where it was at the moment, but was to include the displaced wood in its locality and thus act as a firm link between the two Brigades.

The remainder of the Battalion less 'C' Company, which was still needed in Le Bas de Ranville, was brought up and suitable positions were occupied in what was always known as the Le Mesnil position.

About this time it became painfully obvious that the original plan for the relief of the 6th Airborne Division would have to be modified and that the holding of the bridgehead would continue for much longer than had been expected. The relief Division was at a disadvantage in the bocage country of Normandy and would take a certain time to get accustomed to it, but until they did the Division, and with it the Battalion, would remain in Normandy.

No excitement occurred in the Le Mesnil position, but there was one unfortunate incident which resulted in Lieutenant Thomas being wounded by one of his own sentries as he was returning to his area in the dark, after receiving orders at Battalion HQ. He was hit in the arm and had to be evacuated.

No Battalion ever stays long in a sector where nothing happens and orders were received to relieve a unit of the Airlanding Brigade in the valley of Herouvillette. This unit had recently repulsed a sharp attack, supported by tanks, and was now due for a rest.

"The defence of Herouvillette was complicated by the presence of numerous additional arms which, at first, seemed to be working to their own plans. They were duly incorporated in the defence plan, but were never actually put under our command."

The previous attack had been launched from the direction of Escoville and it seemed more than likely that any further attack would come from the same direction; it was for the most part suitable from the German viewpoint.

'A' Company, under Lt. Parrish, was kept right out of the defence scheme and was retained as a striking force for use when required.

"'C' Company, under Major Bartlett, was in a most imposing looking mansion with stables (empty) and ample grounds, including a training gallop. The place had been a German training college for engineers, but had been left in such a hurry that it was littered with files and fuses and other gadgets for booby traps. There was some anxiety that the place had been booby trapped itself, but this was not so. The exhibits were handed over to the right quarter, where they were of considerable interest, while 'C' Company found some beer in the cellar which interested them too."

Battalion HQ was in a very comfortable residential house with the wife of the owner and her two small sons still in residence. Village gossip was that this woman was a collaborator because one of the instructors from the engineering school had been billeted there for the last three years and they were very friendly with each other. She was an attractive woman and this may have been true, but was more likely to have been just plain gossip.

She told many interesting tales of the occupation and said that Rommel himself had been to Herouvillette only a few weeks before the invasion and had held a conference in her house. He had arrived with a fleet of twelve cars and numerous heel-clicking staff officers. Rommel himself was a red-faced, unhealthy-looking man, who had the complete confidence of his own men, but whose visits were hated because they were always followed by much extra work on the defences. On this occasion he ordered the work to be hastened on the anti-landing obstacles on the DZ and said civilian labour would be used as well as military. The obstacles were trunks of trees about as thick as telegraph poles and twenty feet high; they were planted irregularly about the DZ and some of them were connected to mines. Rommel said they were to be thickened up at once and the spaces between them laced with strands of barbed wire. He was no fool, but gave this order much too late and it was not fully completed at the time of the invasion.

Rommel

The Battalion did not have to wait too long for the next German attempt. The attack was launched at 0400hrs.

"**Almost the first shell struck the side of Battalion HQ, knocking the wall in completely and burying, but not hurting, L/Cpl Emery and Private Strudwick (my batman) and the Second-in-Command. A heavy concentration was directed onto the village generally, but did comparatively little harm as everyone was in their slit trench before it even began. The width of this concentration and the fact that it had begun at a precise time, shortly before dawn, suggested that it would be followed by an infantry attack probably by dawn or just after.**

Soon before dawn 'B' Company reported movement in the wood to their immediate front. No fire was opened up though, but

a close watch was maintained and constant reports were sent back to Battalion HQ."

It was fairly obvious that this movement was infantry forming up for an attack and that the attack would come in from the same direction as before, but care had to be taken that this was not a bluff, with the main attack coming in from another direction altogether.

If the Germans advanced towards 'B' Company, which seemed likely, they would first have to cross a hundred yards of open ground which had been mined by some of their own countrymen. They were almost certainly unaware of the position of 'B' Company and an advance of them would have been more than welcome. The mortars were laid in the wood and artillery called for to stand by to fire on the same target.

"Time passed but the attack did not start. It seemed that the Germans were having to do a bit of sorting out before they could begin. At 8.00am it was decided to make their decision for them and both the mortars and the guns were given the orders to open fire on the wood. There was tremendous confusion in the wood, all watched with great interest by 'B' Company. Germans ran in all directions, some of them coming out towards 'B' Company, only to be picked off by rifle fire."

About the same time enemy tanks were reported in the direction being watched by 'C' Company, but there were anti-tank guns suitably placed to deal with these if they came on. The tanks seemed as undecided as the infantry and moved about at long range, taking no offensive action. The artillery was called on to deal with them and did so with great success, destroying two completely and making the others draw off.

"One very annoying incident occurred when one large tank, which was closing in slowly, was being followed in the sights of a 17-pounder. The gunner was rubbing his hands in anticipation of a certain kill and was just waiting for the best moment to fire, when an armoured car arrived on a routine patrol of the village and also spotted the tank. The car immediately opened fire with its pathetic little 2-pounder which had no effect on the tank except to make it take an interest in the area. The gunner decided to go on waiting, but the decision cost him his life, as the tank, after a short delay, sprayed the whole area with its machine guns. The burst, which was a long one, killed the gunner and his crew."

While all this was happening the Germans facing 'B' Company were showing no signs of attacking and, as there was a chance that they might slip back the way that they had come, a proportion of the artillery was shifted onto a bend in the wood behind them. 'A' Company was ordered to stand by to go in and sort them out.

"A slight difficulty arose at this stage because, although 'A' Company moved right up to their start line and were all ready to go in by 10.30am, it took a full half-hour to stop the artillery from firing. Various extra batteries had been roped in and the gunners were having a grand time. I spent an irritating period on the wireless demanding that all artillery fire cease and eventually it was so. Lt. Parrish was then ordered to take his Company in and clear the wood.

The prisoners were a scruffy looking crowd and, surprisingly, did not include a single officer amongst them. There was, however, a Sergeant Major who, under interrogation, said that the force was a company and that he was in command of it. He added that none of his officers had taken part in the attack, but had done all the planning; he also volunteered his own personal opinion of his officers, which was not a good one.

The wounded of 'A' Company include that very game little officer Lt. McDonald, who was hit seriously in the back and succumbed to his wounds after a terrific fight at the base hospital. The Battalion was in the rest area when he died and all ranks had been following anxiously the struggle for his life. His death came as a great shock as he seemed to be rallying strongly.

This second attack was not followed immediately by another and, as the days went by, it seemed less likely that there would be one and the atmosphere in the village became less tense."

Bob Tanner had joined the 7th Bn and had landed in Normandy. Here he tells us some of his thoughts.

"Normandy - scared? Not really, bloody petrified, the constant shelling, the mortaring, the snipers, men dying around me, wounded. Digging in, the mosquitoes, hard tack biscuits, the patrols, always wondering if we will make it back to base.

The rain, at times so browned off, wondering if we had bitten off more than we could chew. Somehow we came through it. Coming under fire, diving into a ditch running along side the orchard [at Bob's Farm, Chapter 7]. Falling onto a chap, saying sorry, no answer from him, a very dead Gerry.!!

Dashing into the orchard, digging in, more mortaring, didn't Gerry ever run out of the damn things. The stench of death all around."

"Everyone enjoyed their stay at Herouvillette except for the occasion when, through some error, the village was attacked by the RAF using rocket-firing Typhoons. These are certainly the most alarming weapons when you are at the wrong end of them and it was a great relief when they had fired them off and gone away. Fortunately the casualties from this were extremely light; Private Skolly, Medical Orderly from 'A' Company, who was wounded, was the only unlucky one."

The planes were probably meant to have attacked St. Honorine, which lay two miles down the road to the east and was held by the enemy. It was not an important place and it was also covered from several points in the divisional bridgehead; no attempt was ever made to turn them out.

"It was an odd position, though, to have an enemy position right inside the bridgehead and produced some amusing incidents. One of these concerned a line-laying signal detachment from Brigade HQ who approached with their usual chant of *'Line from Brigade HQ where do you want the instrument?'* and were amazed to find a group of German officers seated round a table. The Germans were equally surprised and in the pause that followed the party slipped away.

On another occasion an RASC lorry came touring into Herouvillette just as it was getting dark one evening and pulled up with screaming brakes and locked wheels at the first troops the driver saw. He told an alarming tale of infiltration by large numbers of enemy who were already in the next village; he had seen them for himself and there was no doubt about that. He had taken the wrong road in the failing light and had driven straight through St. Honorine without knowing it."

Chapter Seven

Bob's Farm

As soon as the tension around Herouvillette had relaxed General Gale was able to take action to give some relief to the 3rd Parachute Brigade who were still in the approximate area of their 'Overlord role', covering the east flank of the bridgehead.

The country here was largely forest and bocage, which is merely another name for country of the type familiar to Devonians, as it has the same small fields with thick hedges and sunken roads and can generally be classed as close country. The enemy positions were very close all along this part of the front so that there was a permanent mental strain on the troops. The 3rd Brigade had had a prolonged spell there and had earned their rest so the General decided to relieve them with the 5th Brigade who, not having had the same strain, were less fatigued in mind if not in body.

The Battalion relieved the 8th Battalion in the sector of the front which bordered the Bois de Bavent.

The Bois itself formed the south flank of the position which faced east and was always known as the Bois de Bavent position although it was not in the Bois proper. It was thick forest with a few dead straight roads which mostly ran from east to west and were all parallel to each other. It would be extremely difficult country from which an attack of any size could be launched as control would be almost impossible, but it was ideal country for patrols to move about in.

The ground to the immediate front and to the north of the position was typical bocage country with plenty of cover, but very limited fields of view. The Battalion's neighbours were the 12th Battalion to the north in the area of the crossroads; and a Battalion of the relieving Division was to the south. These latter were in a good position to gain experience of close country fighting which they sought.

As no two Commanders ever have quite the same views of any given problem the positions taken over from the 8th Battalion were not altogether liked and were modified accordingly.

It was not known what strength the enemy were nor had the positions been fixed with any certainty except that they were known to hold positions alongside a double hedgerow and that they also had troops in 'Bob's Farm'. Their supporting troops were thought to be between the hedgerow and La Priere, which might well be their headquarters. They certainly had plenty of mortars as well as the call on a fair number of guns, but whether they consisted of a Battalion or a Company, or even just a few troops put there to contain 7 Para, was anybody's guess and obviously was the first problem to be solved.

"**The Battalion policy was based on two propositions, first that an area which contained the bulk of the Battalion, and was encircled by tracks and the road, was to be regarded as sacred to the Battalion and any German who entered it was to pay with his life or his liberty; and second, that patrol ascendancy was to be obtained from the start.**"

The positions actually manned were, for the most part, slightly in advance of those taken over. As a result a field of fire of sometimes as much as 200 yards, but in most cases only about 100 yards, was secured for the forward troops.

"Gaining of patrol ascendancy was an interesting game and was tackled systematically and with great enthusiasm by all concerned. The intelligence section, under the indefatigable Lieutenant Mills, worked literally day and night and prepared in the first instance a large-scale map of the whole Battalion area and went as far as La Priere. Known features were given code names for easy reference but, as some of these were unprintable, they cannot be repeated here. The maps of the area were fairly good, but proved inaccurate in several smaller details, so the quite excellent air photos, which had been issued to 'Overlord', were used for reference in making the sketch map. There were, quite naturally, a great number of blank bits at first. In fact the original was little more than an outline, but as time went on it got more and more detailed. I ordered that nothing was to be included which was not known for certain to be accurate, as the whole patrol policy would be laid down from this map.

The earlier patrols were nearly all sent out with the object of collecting topographical information. They always went out at night and as they were not required to get information about the enemy, and had been ordered to avoid contact with him, they gained valuable experience of patrolling in bocage country without suffering casualties in the gaining of it. This, in its turn, produced added confidence and a thorough personal knowledge of the ground in front.

Information about the enemy and the location of his chief positions was gained by the lookouts in the forward posts, who were, in many cases, within 100 yards of similar German posts.

The Battalion snipers really came into their own and would disappear to the east for the whole day with their pockets stuffed with chocolate and biscuits and return in the evening with several new notches on their rifles. One of the most disappointed men in the whole Battalion was a Private from 'B' Company who was a sniper, he came back after his first day without a notch on his rifle. He had had a German in his sights soon after he got into his position, but he had not fired as the range was only 300 yards and he 'was after the longer stuff'. He was unlucky and did not get another target that day, although he made up for it later. These snipers, in addition to picking off several Germans themselves, kept the enemy in a state of continual suspense and usually brought back with them useful information of enemy positions and relief systems.

The enemy, for their part, were not completely inactive either and certainly carried out a number of patrols that we knew nothing about and which resulted in them learning the location of some of the positions. Practically every one of our positions seen had an alternative one and many of them had more than one; though despite these precautions casualties were suffered from the shelling and the mortaring which went on, intermittently, most of the time.

An effective counter mortar system was operated through Brigade HQ and, after a few teething troubles, became most effective. As soon as an enemy mortar or gun opened up on any part of the Brigade front the telephone lines would hum with compass

The Tale of Two Bridges

bearings and other details and within five minutes the enemy themselves would be getting back three bombs for every one they sent over."

The systematic search for information went on steadily and by and by sufficient data had been collected to warrant an offensive on a known position with a view to collecting prisoners to supplement, and check, the information already obtained.

The objective was a farmhouse known to be occupied by the Germans. 'B' Company were to carry out the raid and the farm was christened 'Bob's Farm' after Major Keene who would be leading the raid and Major Keene's own account is the best way of describing it.

"After a few days I had rather a secure feeling being in the reserve position and hearing the stories of the goings on in the forward companies, but my tune soon changed when I heard that 'B' was to take part in a little party slightly to the front of 'A' position. Teddy Poole (Lt. Poole) had been up in this area with a strong patrol in search of some mortar positions which had given us a good deal of trouble and it was decided that a company should go up and sort the thing out.

Bob Keene

After a recce one morning, coupled with information from the sappers, the Commanding Officer roughed out a plan and when the finer details had been attended to it was much as follows.

After a good stink from the Light Regiment RA, 'B' Company and a small party of sappers, commanded by Lieutenant Forster, would go in, the objective being a farmhouse and a double hedgerow and a few cottages in the rear of the farm. We had also to have a look at some ominous looking pits which were thought to be mortar pits. When the barrage started, the Company moved up the only approach, a deep gully leading right up to the farm, and as the shelling stopped we moved to our left along a low hedgerow which was to be the start line; this was all effected and things were running smoothly.

The Tale of Two Bridges

From the start line one could clearly see the farm building about seventy yards away. When the covering guns were in position I gave the order for the Company to get in, the drill being to put two Platoons in first and follow up with the third, but nothing happened so I yelled out again. It seemed most strange and for a moment I could not understand what had happened; there was very little going on in the way of shooting. What the hell could it be? My runner, Private Cornell, then pointed out that someone was coming down from the direction of the left hand Platoon and looked rather like one of the runners, but when the body got nearer it proved to be Teddy Poole, who informed me that a Boche Platoon was forming up at the end of our start and it looked as if they were going to attack us. This was a bit annoying especially coming at such an awkward time, the barrage had been down for at least five minutes and I was beginning to wonder when the Boche were going to open up in all seriousness.

As time was an important factor, I yelled out orders to the Company as they lay behind the start line. To my complete amazement everything worked like a charm. The orders were roughly as follows - left hand Platoon will take the Boche Platoon at the end of our start line - right hand Platoon will move up to the position of the left hand Platoon - reserve Platoon and Company HQ will take the place of the right hand Platoon - MOVE!

In a few minutes everyone was in position and off we went. The Platoon commanded by Poole was to rejoin us when we were in the farm area. The Company maintained a very good open formation across the orchard towards the farm and all of us were peering through trees for holes in the walls through which we were to go. This information had come from a Sapper source and we were a bit disappointed when we saw that these holes did not exist, but in their place was one ordinary five-barred gate leading into the farm from the orchard, this was closed.

I would not like to suggest whose fault it was that I had the pleasure of opening that gate, something to do with the excellent formation we keep, no doubt. However, once inside the farmyard the two Platoons got cracking and cleared it up. Fortunately only a few Boche were encountered and, after a quick re-organisation, we set off in the direction of the supposed mortar pits. Just as we were moving off

Poole's Platoon came in and all they had to say was, 'Mr. Poole's had it Sir, got hit by a mortar bomb'. This was rather final news and so we got on to the next objective from the start line."

Tommy Farr (Lt. Farr) was with the leading Platoon in this phase and he certainly got cracking.

As I came up the road, Boche prisoners were coming in and there were a large number of stiffs lying around. We reached the so-called mortar pits and, to our dismay, they were not pits at all but large craters caused by the Typhoons who had beaten the place up with their rockets. At this stage we came under very heavy fire and for a few minutes were completely pinned down. The fire came from the direction of the double hedges, therefore clearing this part was definitely not on and it was even a bit tricky getting back to the farm.

At this stage Tommy Farr stopped one through the hand, but kept going and got his Platoon in. The area round the farm was very close and observation was poor and what with the casualties and one thing and another the Company did not appear very strong. A number of prisoners had been taken back, under escort, and as their capture was one of the important factors they were well escorted; a number of our own casualties were also carried back by men of the Company and more chaps were still wandering around, but at the time I had a feeling that the Company had incurred heavy casualties.

Once back at the farm I tried to contact my Company Sergeant Major (CSM), Durbin, who had taken the rest of Company HQ up the gully with orders to meet me in the farm. The reason for this was that I did not want to take certain personnel in the assault with me and left the CSM to act as Second-in-Command of the Company, and he had with him the normal reps a Second-in-Command would have had. I had a Second-in-Command at the time, thus in this way if Company HQ 'went for a burton' then he could take over. Of his party few were to be seen and I then learned that the CSM had been killed, he was hit by either a splinter or a bullet and wounded and then he took on an LMG position and in this gallant way he met his death. As the gun was still active it was impossible to get his body and recover it, although gallant attempts were made by Corporal Bartle and Private Weston.

At this stage I decided to hold the farm until everyone was in and all the casualties had been evacuated, I also had a strong feeling that a counter attack might be launched at any moment. During this time the Boche were pretty active with their mortars and gave the whole area a good showering. It was about this time that the Company had its first experience of what we later called a 'Moaning Minnie', a multi-barrelled mortar which earned the full respect of all concerned, the most unpleasant thing about this weapon was the terrifying noise the missiles made when they were under way.

After a brief check up on the positions around the farm I returned to Company HQ which was in the actual farmhouse and there I met Sergeant Harper who informed me that Mr. Poole was not dead and with any luck he would pull through. This was great news and I later heard that Poole was back at the MDS, but had lost a foot. After a final check up with the aid of Sergeants Harper and Bettle I gave orders for the remainder of 'B' to get out using the gully as the best line of withdrawal. This move went quite well and I am sure it coincided with a rather half-hearted counter attack put in by the Boche.

"The gully afforded very good cover indeed as it was ten to twenty foot deep, but needless to say it was very well ranged by the Germans who made it quite unpleasant. With me in the last party I had Sergeant Harper and Bettle, Private Purdy, a signaller who had lost his 68 set (wireless), Private Davis one of the MT and a non parachutist, who acted as my runner throughout, and Private Green. About half way back along the gully we came across Captain Parrish's (Commanding Officer of 'A' Company) Private Humble, who had been badly wounded in both legs. There was little we could do for him except administer the usual shot of Morphia, although we did try to move him it was obviously impossible without medical attention and the aid of a stretcher. It was a difficult moment as I was very reluctant to leave him there, but it was impossible to move him, so I decided that as we were then within seventy yards or so of 'A' Company's forward positions, a stretcher party would have to go out as soon as we contacted 'A' Company."

This was not all though and having gone another twenty yards I stumbled over a body lying in the bottom of the gully and turned back to see who it was. To my horror I found it was Walter Parrish. He was badly wounded and had lost a lot of blood, but was still conscious; he told me that as so many chaps seemed to be filtering back, he thought that perhaps things had taken a turn for the worse and he was on his way up to see if he could give me a hand when a shower from a 'Moaning Minnie' had caught him and his runner Private Humble. Here I was confronted with the same problem, medical attention and stretcher bearers were urgently needed. And then, by the grace of God, Private Liddell and a stretcher party turned up. There was a wounded Boche lying on top of the gully on a stretcher. In a short time Captain Parrish and Private Humble were on the stretchers and the Boche fuming because he had been dropped to priority three. He was later brought in.

When the party passed through the forward positions of 'A' Company I met RSM Johnson, who had done, and was still doing, great work getting the casualties out and passing them back to the RAP. So to all intents and purposes the raid was over, three officers were wounded, my CSM killed and there had been other casualties that I was not aware of. Certainly more of the Company had been wounded and killed. On arriving at Battalion HQ I met the CO and told him roughly what had happened. To my surprise he stopped me and told me what had happened. Our views were very different, but the peculiar thing was that his story was the correct one! He obviously knew more about these things than I did.

RSM Johnson, MBE, MM

When back in the Company area I met Sergeant Prentice who was to take the place of my late CSM. He had not actually taken part in the raid, but had done very good work in preparing for our return, as had also my CQMS Bush. I went round the Company to check the CO's story and found that we had three killed and about a dozen wounded. I could hardly believe it, but it was the best news I had had for a long time. For the casualties we incurred in the raid was merited; some 30 Boche had been killed and others wounded and a family of intact prisoners had been captured."

"**The prisoners, under interrogation, revealed several very interesting bits of news. One of these was that the Germans were**

The Tale of Two Bridges

themselves planning a rather similar type of operation against the Battalion position which was scheduled to take place the next day. The prisoner did not think that it would now take place. He was quite right it did not.

The sector was eventually handed back to the 8th Battalion and the Battalion moved back for its first spell in the rest area.

The Divisional Rest Area (DRA) was as far from the enemy as it could be, while still remaining in the bridgehead, but this meant that it was close to the bridges which were a target for the nightly bombing attacks. It was also the gun position area of the Division.

It was a bit too noisy, especially at night, to be really restful, but the feeling of being out of actual contact with the enemy was a rest in itself which was much appreciated by all. No one did very much beyond changing their clothes and lazing about and perhaps writing a few letters, but in a few days all feeling of fatigue had worn off and the Battalion was ready for further action.

One very sad but important job was started during this first spell in the Rest Area and maintained not only throughout the campaign covered by this account, but right up to the time of writing. A simple wooden cross was made by the Battalion carpenter, Private Hardwick, for the fallen. All these were lettered by Sergeant Smith, the signal Sergeant, who was also an expert signwriter. A standard cross for the Battalion thus came into being which, although by necessity [was] very simple, was at the same

"...bodies were later exhumed by the War Graves Commission and re-buried in the 6th Airborne Division Cemetery at Ranville in Normandy, where the Division landed on D-Day"

The Tale of Two Bridges

Major John Went
Company Commander

time both neat and dignified. A Parachute Regiment cap badge was fixed near the top of each, with the distinctive green backing peculiar to the Battalion. Captain Went (later promoted to Major), the Administrative Officer, was put in charge of burials generally and, from the very start, the Battalion was proud of the fact that the graves of their particular comrades were always amongst the neatest and best tended of the whole Division."

As time went on these crosses became landmarks by which the route of the Battalion's advance from Normandy to deep into Germany itself could be followed.

The gaps in the ranks were partially filled by the arrival of a draft of three officers and one hundred reinforcements. These were not trained parachutists, or even parachute volunteers, so that their arrival, although more than welcome, caused some despondency in the ranks and in the mind of Pine-Coffin... **"It seemed possible that our parachuting days were over. We were to get more and more non-parachuting reinforcements and would finish the campaign as ordinary infantry.**

The draft were all from the KSLI except the officers. Two of these were Canadians, Lieutenants Patterson and Pape, while the third, Lieutenant Howard, was English. They were all first class material and very quickly fitted into the Battalion, absorbing the spirit which they found there. It is interesting to note that, when the time for a decision came, they were so much part and parcel of the Battalion that over 80% of the survivors volunteered for parachuting and so accompanied the Battalion to the end of its operations."

Lt 'Pat' Patterson
Platoon Commander

The Battalion returned to its previous position on the Bois and much the same sort of existence as before was followed.

The Divisional policy was to remain on the defensive, as there was nothing to be gained by extending the perimeter of the bridgehead and thus making it harder to hold. At the same time it was important not to give this impression to the enemy and so encourage him to take the initiative. The patrol programme was an active one which started to keep the enemy in a state of anxiety as well as to prevent him from returning the favour.

"It was decided to push the whole bridgehead forward by one tactical feature. This meant, of course, in nearly every case, moving the main position forward to the next hedge in front, where the outposts had been before. The large-scale map was of great assistance here and enabled the various moves to be planned very carefully and all the men thoroughly briefed before any attempts were made.

All the moves took place successfully and without casualties, except on the extreme right of the Battalion sector which bordered the Bois proper. Here No. 9 Platoon of 'C' Company, when advancing to occupy the new position, came under fire from an unexpected direction and lost Lieutenant R. Atkinson the Commander and Private Trafford, both of whom were killed.

The casualty rate amongst the officers had been very high and the loss of Atkinson deprived the Battalion of its last original rifle Platoon Commander.

After the completion of the moves 'C' Company were facing the Germans across a field not more than 100 yards wide, on the right, while on the left 'B' Company had moved up to within 250 yards of 'Bob's Farm'. These new positions were covered as soon as possible by protective wire, which was put up at night and in the greatest silence. No casualties were suffered in carrying out this unpleasant but necessary duty and the presence of the wire helped relieve the mental strain on the men in the most forward positions especially at night.

'B' Company very soon found that a PIAT suitably cocked up at their new position could lob bombs into 'Bobs Farm'; there was no shortage of bombs, so a large number were sent over at different times. The PIAT was most spectacular in this role, as the bomb could be seen all the way to the target where the explosion would blow the roof tiles as much as twenty feet into the air, with great sheets of flame behind them. Visitors to the area were nearly always taken forward for a demonstration of this novelty and some very senior officers were found to be not above firing off a few bombs themselves. It is doubtful if it produced any very concrete results as the number of Germans in the farm, at any time, was limited. Those that were there though must have had a very unpleasant tour of duty. Each visit to the Bois was to be marked by some venture of a rather more elaborate nature than usual. On the first occasion it was the raid on 'Bob's Farm' to get prisoners for interrogation and this time it was the prisoners that were wanted again.

The Battalion was to locate a suitable objective and make all preparations for a raid which would be carried out by a small party from the Twenty-Second Independent Parachute Company. It was finally decided to pinch out the position known to be at the south end of the line marked x-y on the sketch map. [No copy is available.]

The plan was a simple one of bluff. There was to be a certain amount of activity across the whole Battalion front, but with just a few indications to make the German Commander suspect an attack on the right of his front. The raiding party would then slip in quickly on the left.

At the time of the raid the wind was blowing gently and steadily direct from the German positions and in the faces of 'C' Company, making it possible to use smoke as an aid. This had been hoped for, but was so dependent on weather conditions that it could not be relied upon. 'Bob's Farm' and the positions near it on the right of the German front were treated to a good quantity of smoke, liberally laced with high explosive (HE), in accordance with the bluff, and produced the desired result. Practically every German machine gun in that immediate area opened up and kept on firing until the smoke cleared. With any luck they may have shot some of their own men in the muddle. A much smaller amount of smoke and HE was put down at the same time at other points on this front and a two-inch mortar was carefully ranged on a point ten yards inside the chosen objective. HE was used for this ranging which was carried out most carefully until bombs could be dropped, with certainty, almost exactly on the spot required.

At 1.50pm two smoke bombs were fired from the two-inch mortar and so, with the smoke screen on one side and a hedge on the other, this made good cover. There was a German position at the far end of this corridor and the raiding party of 'C' Company's end. The raiding party could move up this corridor unseen by the enemy.

The party consisted of seven members of the Independent Parachute Company and was commanded by Lieutenant R. de Lateur of the same Company. De Lateur had had the distinction of being the first allied soldier to set foot in Normandy as he commanded the leading Platoon of the pathfinder force and had jumped as number one from the leading aircraft.

The raid went exactly as planned and the enemy were completely surprised; they were, in fact, facing to their right as had been hoped and three of them were collected alive and were doubled back to 'C' Company positions. Although completely successful in its object the raid did entail more shooting; there was a brisk exchange of shots, at close range, mostly with submachine guns, before the prisoners were collected. During this de Lateur was hit just above the heart. The stretcher bearers who went with the raiding party got him back very quickly but, nevertheless, he died in the Regimental Aid Post and, with him, The Independent Company lost its last surviving officer.

The prisoners were sent back to Brigade HQ for interrogation, but before they went they were first questioned by the Battalion Intelligence Officer for information of particular importance to the Battalion. Lieutenant Mills, in addition to being the Intelligence Officer, was also a fluent German speaker and possessed the knack of getting facts out of prisoners. This ability was of tremendous value because there is no doubt that most prisoners are frightened soon after capture, but gain confidence as time goes by. If they can be asked a few really searching questions as soon as they come in, the chances of getting some really useful information are very high indeed. It was so with these three prisoners and proved to be so on many future occasions."

After this brief spell of action the Battalion handed over once more to the 8th Battalion and returned to the rest area for another spell, but soon they were back in the same places in the now very familiar Bois. Everyone got used to existence in the Bois by this time and, although the strain was as great as ever, a tendency grew for men to take undue risks, due no doubt either to over confidence or to boredom. This was a very gratifying fault, but a fault all the same which could well cause loss of life, so steps had to be taken to stop it.

"A not unamusing example was provided by Corporal Wilson and Private Butterwood, of 'C' Company, who occupied the right hand forward position. These two developed the habit of carrying out unofficial daylight patrols together by moving up the lane towards the German positions and lying up in the hopes of capturing an unwary Boche. One day Butterwood, for some reason, was not ready to start with Wilson, who set off alone. Our positions and the enemy's were only 100 yards apart and the Germans had felled a tree across the lane about 30 yards from their end to give them cover from observation.

Wilson, with his Sten gun slung across his back to get past this obstacle, had just done so when he was horrified to see two German soldiers swing into the lane from their end. All three were taken aback and none was in a position to do anything about it as the Germans also had their weapons slung. One of them, a large man, had a Schmeisser machine carbine and the other [had] a rifle. It is quite a slow business to unsling a weapon, to cock it and then fire and there is always the chance that the other man may be quicker at it than you are, so none made the attempt. Wilson was on the wrong side of the tree and so could not conveniently disappear and the Germans were not much better placed themselves. A dumb charade then took place with Wilson beckoning the Germans to come forward to him and surrender and they solemnly shaking their heads in refusal and then beckoning Wilson over to them, which invitation he also refused. The impasse might have lasted indefinitely had not the smaller German, the one with the rifle, suddenly turned tail and bolted up the lane. This broke the tension and the meeting dispersed hurriedly."

The Tale of Two Bridges

The question of breaking out of the divisional bridgehead was exercising the higher command at this time and plans were made on a high level to gauge both the enemy's strength and his determination to hang on. There was the possibility that the enemy had only a small number of troops employed as a mere containing force. It was decided to launch an attack, through the Battalion's position, push the enemy out of theirs and occupy it instead. The enemy's reaction to this would provide the answer to the question. The 13th Battalion, who had been in Brigade reserve, were given the task and pulled right back behind the bridges for special training. For various reasons this attack never came off. Instead the 7th Battalion was required to carry out a similar show but on a smaller scale.

"**[I] was most anxious not to maroon one Company in what might well prove to be a hornets' nest, especially as this Company would have to expect casualties before it even got there. This point was accepted by General Gale who agreed that the operation should take the form of a raid on a company scale. The sooner it could be carried out the better because there had already been considerable delay before the 13th Battalion's effort had been called off.**

'Bob's Farm' **was the ideal objective, but this had been done before and the enemy would be alert. Time was short, however, and the specially intensive patrolling that was done failed to find a really suitable objective on the other flank. It was decided, somewhat reluctantly, to carry out a modification of the original** 'Bob's Farm' **raid and to carry this out in daylight. The job fell to** 'B' **Company who would be able to profit from their experience of the first raid."**

The plan generally was to occupy the farm and then, covered by a party remaining in the farm area, swing right handed and sweep clean across the German front line, killing or capturing all the Germans in it. It was probable that this would test their reactions. The capture of the farm was to be assisted by artillery, mortar and PIAT fire, while the sweep along the front would be covered by small arms fire from 'C' Company's forward positions. Every automatic weapon in the Battalion, together with six captured German machine guns, was brought forward for this job. The volume of fire available was terrific and a very careful plan had to be evolved to keep the fire just ahead of 'B' Company and to prevent accidents. 'B' Company's leading troops would throw out smoke grenades at intervals to show how far they had got and no gun was to fire beyond the left of a line straight to its front. Advance Battalion HQ would be in 'C' Company's forward positions from which it could observe and control things.

"Just before the raid was due to begin there was a slight set back. The Germans managed to work some men forward into 'C' Company's forward positions, which consisted of a long hedgerow and was normally occupied by one Platoon only. A confused battle, which might have gone on indefinitely, took place in this hedgerow. The situation had to be cleared up quickly if the raid was to take place. Major Bartlett, commanding 'C' Company, was ordered to take the hedge at once with another Platoon. This he duly did and at great speed, but in the resulting shooting he himself was wounded and had to be evacuated. Command of 'C' Company was assumed by Captain Woodman, the only officer left in it, who was later confirmed in the appointment and duly promoted."

Captain Eric Woodman

The raid began at 4pm with Lieutenant Pape's Platoon on the right moving up the gully and another Platoon commanded by Sergeant Ricketts up the lane on the left. There was no third Platoon in 'B' Company at this time. Company HQ followed Pape's Platoon up the gully.

The first leg of the plan was a simple pincer movement, covered by artillery, mortar and PIAT fire and aimed to capture the farm itself.

"Sergeant Ricketts' Platoon got held up almost at once and could thereafter only assist with fire. Pape worked his way steadily up the gully, from which it could be seen that the farm had been sandbagged and had a lookout in a sandbagged position on the roof. The gully was only passable for part of the way as the Germans had filled in the bottom of it, at their end, with some coils of barbed wire. Sergeant Norman, commanding the leading section, did wonders to get as far as he did, but finally had to report that he could get no further. Even as this news reached Major Keene four men were caught in booby traps just in front of his HQ.

Keene decided to leave the gully and rush for the farm across the open using Pape's Platoon and his own HQ party with the object of getting a footing in the farm as quickly as possible. He had Le Cheminant, a signaller, with him with a 38 set which was netted to [my] 68 set at Advanced Battalion HQ. These two checked at the brick wall, near to the same gate that Keene had had to open himself on the first raid, and sent a report back.

Meanwhile Pape's Platoon, together with CSM Prentice, Private Cornell the runner and Private Arnold Butler, Major Keene's batman, rushed through the gate and into the farm. All hell was let loose for a few minutes, but soon it was in their hands with some valuable prisoners. These prisoners included four German stretcher bearers whose leader spoke English and immediately put himself and his men at the disposal of the attackers; they did extremely good work during the raid for wounded of both sides.

Major Keene had the bad luck to tread on a shoe mine soon after he passed his message and was on his way to the farm. He was seriously wounded about the leg and was later evacuated.

He remained in control at the time though, but was, of course, completely immobilised. He planned to keep Pape's Platoon in the farm area until Sergeant Ricketts' Platoon arrived to put Pape onto phase two of the raid. Ricketts' Platoon being pinned at the other side of the front naturally did not arrive at all, but instead the Germans reacted very strongly to the attention that had been paid to them and opened up on the farm with everything that they had, which was far more than had been expected.

It was at once clear that the original plan would have to be modified. Fortunately, Brigadier Poett was with [me] at Advanced Battalion HQ and he immediately authorised the withdrawal of the raiding party. The withdrawal was far from easy because of the very heavy mortar fire which the Germans were then putting down and because of two German machine gunners who fired continuously down the gully from the farm and as soon as the last troops vacated it. These gunners were largely neutralised by the extremely gallant action of Sergeant Lucas who posted himself, with a Bren gun, by a tree half-way up the bank of the gully. Lucas fired his Bren standing and deliberately drew fire onto himself by engaging the Germans with his Bren. Under cover of this the raiding party, together with their casualties, managed to slip out and it is good to report that Lucas eventually got himself out unscathed. This was one of the many fine acts by Lucas throughout the campaign; he proved himself to be an outstanding soldier in action. The small arms covering fire from 'C' Company's position was carried out during the withdrawal and succeeded in drawing some of the shelling and mortaring away from the gully. A Lance Corporal who was with the intelligence section who was with Advanced Battalion HQ was killed by a shell during this stage. The Germans continued to pound the area for some hours after the raid was over and seemed to think that something significant was afoot; they also treated different parts of the divisional area to shelling at the same time.

Those who took part in the raid were disappointed at the results obtained as it appeared that little had been achieved. General Gale, however, was most emphatic that it had been 100% successful and had given him exactly the information that he required. He now knew, he said, that the enemy intended to hold that area tightly, were in considerable strength and were extremely touchy about the whole thing. This was proved by the volume of ammunition they were prepared to expend on what was really only a small-scale offensive."

In brief the raid for 'Bob's Farm' had seen 'B' Company passing through 'A' Company under heavy mortar fire. 'B' Company then moved up a narrow gully with two actions on a path to the north. The two actions on the path were pinned down at once and the remainder of the Company in the gully got into trouble with booby traps. The gully was waist deep in water and found to be full of anti-personnel mines. Major Keene being wounded by stepping on one. In this raid, which gained valuable information, Major Keene, Lieutenant Patterson and 20 other ranks were wounded and 3 other ranks were killed, Lance Corporal Coulthard, Price and Private Evans.

They were buried at Ranville on July 11th.

The Tale of Two Bridges

The Battalion at the end of this period in the Bois was given another demonstration of the weight of German artillery and mortars. The day before the Battalion was due to be relieved a very heavy artillery concentration was brought down in the area of Battalion HQ, but the slit trenches were good and casualties were remarkably light. This artillery concentration proved to be only the first of many and the area was kept under almost continuous fire for six and a half hours. At times the noise rose to a crescendo when the shelling was added to by a great number of mortars, all firing rapid, and 'Moaning Minnies', the multi-barrelled rocket projectors.

"It was very flattering to be selected for so much attention but, as time went on and no infantry attack was launched, the reason for it became more and more of a mystery. Sleep was out of the question for anyone so there was no problem about keeping alert. Everyone expected a sudden cessation of fire followed by the appearance of a number of hot and excited German soldiers, complete with bayonets and the will to win, but these never came and finally the dawn appeared instead and with it everything returned to normal once more. It seemed that some kind of attack was started against the unit on our right flank and the firing which landed on the Battalion was intended to cut off the crossroads just in our rear. Supplies and reinforcements would normally have had to pass the crossroads. The attack was not pressed home and was, in fact, a complete failure which must have cost the Reich a great deal of money without gaining them a thing."

This was the Battalion's last visit to the Bois and it was right and proper that it should be the most exciting of them all. There were two other events of interest during the period which may bear relating.

The big attack for the capture of Caen took place during this period and the Bois was an excellent position from which to watch, as well as being close enough to intercept the tank Commanders' wireless conversations. Everyone had read of the thousand-bomber raids that had been taking place all over Germany, but in the night before the attack, just before dark, all ranks were able to watch 500 British bombers unloading their bombs on the selected part of the town. It was a most impressive sight. It was particularly interesting to watch the work of the little Auster artillery spotting planes which also took to the air and prevented many of the German flak batteries from engaging the bombers. The flak batteries knew that as soon as they gave their positions away to the spotter he would bring the ground artillery onto them with very great accuracy.

The other event concerned Captain Fortnum, the Quartermaster, and some planes of the RAF. The Quartermaster had set up in the brickworks just in the rear of the Battalion position and here he took pride in keeping the whole of his area clean and tidy, despite the shells and mortar bombs which were frequently dropped on him. All the cooking was done in this area and parties came out of the Bois for a hot wash when they could be relieved. It was a very pleasant place and reflected great credit on all those who worked there. One night two planes carrying leaflets intended for the Germans made an error of judgement and showered the spotless brickyard with thousands of leaflets explaining, in German, that the Wehrmacht was not really doing very well and was bound to be beaten before long. Those fell on the roof as well as all over the yard and the place was never quite the same again afterwards. This little incident annoyed the Quartermaster and his minions far more than the really huge bombs which had been dropped a few days before by the Germans and very nearly wiped out the whole Battalion.

Capt Reg Fortnum
Quartermaster

The Tale of Two Bridges

Chapter Eight

The Break Out

The Battalion's next move was to a completely new part of the bridgehead - the northeast corner of it. Here, in a village called Hauger, the Battalion led a varied existence.

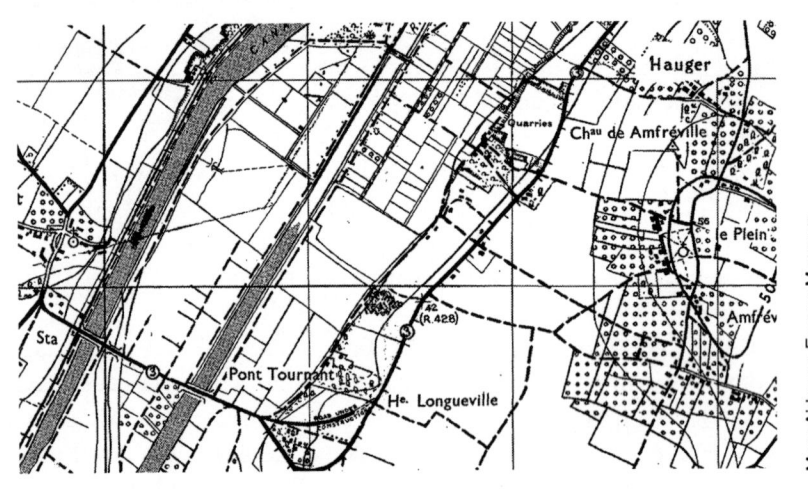

Map: Airborne Forces Museum

Brigade Headquarters was also in the village and the bulk of the positions were a full mile from the enemy. The accommodation was good and it seemed that the location alone would be a tonic after the Bois.

There was a rude shock though when, as the move in was actually taking place, a shell struck the house, which was being occupied as a regimental aid post. Several casualties were suffered from this unlucky shot. Curiously no further shelling was experienced at all and on one occasion George Formby (a popular entertainer at the time) and his wife Beryl gave an impromptu performance in a field just behind Brigade Headquarters. On the whole life was fairly pleasant for the bulk of the Battalion who were screened from direct contact with the enemy by an isolated wood to their front.

"This wood was a most unpleasant spot and was occupied for 24 hours at a time by one Platoon. Conditions there were very similar to those of the Bois, only rather more so as the Germans facing the position were of a more adventurous type. They had the habit of crawling up the edge of the wood itself, which was a comparatively easy task in the long grass, and throwing hand grenades into it. To add to the troubles of the Platoon in this wood there existed enormous numbers of mosquitoes, which made it impossible to eat or to talk without swallowing several of them.

George Formby entertained the troops

Patrolling was as active as ever and as a result of it German positions were accurately located and charted. These positions were very well sighted making it difficult to attack one without coming under fire from at least one other. Lieutenant Howard, who had joined the Battalion in the rest area, failed to return from one of these patrols and was presumed killed; together with three members of his patrol."

Altogether it was an unsatisfactory position and everyone was pleased when the whole Brigade pulled out of the line and went into the Ranville area.

The Battalion was given good accommodation in the Le Bois de Ranville and immediately got down to the administrative problems which had hitherto, by force of circumstance, been of low priority. Billets were thoroughly scrubbed out, to the complete agreement of the owners, and every item of equipment was very thoroughly inspected.

"Brigadier Poett carried out an administrative inspection and a REME team inspected the vehicles and instruments at the same time. The resulting report was a good one. The greatest credit for this was due to Private Lewis, the water duty man and driver of the Battalion water truck. This cart, though it had been new at

The Tale of Two Bridges

the start of the operation, was in continual use throughout. Never once was anyone short of his ration of water; day after day whatever the conditions the water cart would invariably get up with Lewis at the wheel. Which everyone gave him full marks for, for keeping it running at all. The REME team awarded the water cart 100% in their report which meant that this team of experts were unable to find a single fault with any part of the cart; this they admitted represented an outstanding feat of maintenance on the part of Lewis."

The checking of the equipment and the leisurely life led by the Battalion gave rise to the usual crop of rumours. The most popular, and the strongest one, was that the Division was going home. All the rumours proved to be false, as was usually the case, and on August 12th the Battalion was put on an hour's notice to move. There was a certain vagueness about where the move would end, but it was obviously something pretty big as the whole Division was to take part. The Battalion was to move to an area a few miles south of the old Bois position and there await orders for further movement to the east. This was to be the breakout from the divisional bridgehead for which everyone had been waiting for so long. By the 17th the Battalion was in this jumping off position when orders were received from the Brigadier.

"There were indications that the Germans were pulling out of their positions and preparing to retire eastwards and the Division was going to follow them up. 3rd Parachute Brigade was to lead and the 5th Brigade would be passed through them in due course. The immediate route through Escoville, from which attacks on Herouvillette had twice been launched, and then on through Troarn to the east. The final destination was unknown, but the maximum speed would be maintained to keep the Germans on the run.

A glance at the map was sufficient to show that this was not going to be so very simple. The whole country seemed to be covered with rivers and all of these ran across the line of advance. Bridges were sure to be blown and the Germans would be certain to fight delaying tactics at each river."

As expected, opposition was encountered by 5 and 3 Brigades and also, as expected, the enemy slipped back hastily to the next river and were prepared to fight a delaying action under favourable conditions. The 3rd Brigade had been checked into an area which overlooked the river and 5 Brigade was moved up and grouped just short of the village.

"It was more than likely that the 5th Brigade would be used for a crossing of the river that night, so the various Commanders made considerable use of the village church tower as a vantage point. This tower had already been practically demolished by shellfire and was a very obvious target for German guns. But was, on the other hand, quite the best observation point in the village. No casualties were suffered in it although it was frequently shelled. It just happened that no-one was using it at the time. A great deal of luck enters into such matters not only at this stage but also in the action which followed during the night."

From the tower it was possible to see not only a good stretch of the river itself but also most of the approach to it. This was broken country in which it would be difficult to maintain direction in the dark. It was not possible to say, at this stage, what part of the river the Battalion would be making for. So all that could be done was to get a general view of the type of country involved and to memorise the more outstanding landmarks.

While the Commanders were busy at the tower, the remainder of the Battalion was having a very pleasant rest in orchards and fields just short of the village itself, while the Quartermaster and cooks produced hot meals as if they were in the barracks. But things were about to get busy again.

"Towards evening the Brigadier got the expected orders and was able to give the outline of his plan, though he was unable to go into much detail as conditions of the possible river crossing places were unknown, as the 3rd Brigade was still fighting down to them. There were three bridges by which infantry might be able to cross under the cover of darkness and one of these was allotted to each Battalion. The 7th was given the middle one."

The Tale of Two Bridges

The broad plan was for the 12th Battalion on the right to attack the village on the far bank, Putot en Auge, at dawn the following morning. The 7th Battalion was to move up at the same time on their left flank to a line just beyond the village, when the 13th Battalion would be passed through the 7th and capture the high ground which dominated the river.

"Start times, forming up places, routes of advance and all the other details considered so vital in the planning of even the smallest of night operations had, by necessity, to be dealt with in the most sketchy way. Great use had to be made of the map, which certainly would not be completely accurate in the smaller details. The points at which the river would actually be crossed could not be laid down for certain until the state of the bridges was known. Other details could not be given at all and it was certain that further orders would be received over the wireless once the advance had begun. A complete alteration of the original plan was not unlikely. In theory the Brigade was tackling the impossible and nothing but muddle could result. In practice, however, no-one even considered failure and the ghastly possibilities of muddles in the night, with Battalions shooting each other up, only occurred to a very few. The river had to be crossed that night and the plan was bound to rely on a certain amount of luck.

The advance was difficult as various unseen obstacles, particularly impenetrable hedges, were encountered on the way and wide detours had to be made. The enemy was suspicious and constantly shot up flares which made the troops on the ground feel very exposed, but at the same time helped the advance by showing up certain landmarks. The usual fixed line machine guns were also fired at intervals at what the Germans considered likely places. They were very good at picking out these places and had most bottlenecks and gates well covered, but they made their usual mistake of using tracer ammunition so that the line of the gun could easily be seen and that area avoided. Lieutenant Mills as usual did an excellent job of leading the Battalion through the night and getting round many obstacles without actually losing direction. The silent passage of an obstacle such as a hedge by a large number of fully equipped men in the dark is a slow and difficult business and as a result the Battalion was not on its start line until one hour later than had been hoped."

Various modifications of the plan had been notified over the wireless, but unfortunately did not materially alter the role of the Battalion. They chiefly concerned the 13th Battalion who had been trying to cross the river by a blown bridge, well to the left of the Battalion (7 Para). They had found that this bridge was completely uncrossable even to the infantry and had been ordered to come back and try another point closer in. This meant that the Battalion would be expected to be seen somewhere to the 13th Battalion's left, at some point of the proceedings, and would require careful watching if accidents were to be avoided, especially if the contact was made in the dark or half light. The Battalion crossed the railway line in the station area at dawn and immediately had difficulty in finding the track which was its line of further advance. The map was completely at fault here and showed a track leading from the station in exactly the direction required.

"No such track existed on the ground and some time was wasted in searching for it and in finally moving up the hedgerow which ran in the same direction.

'B' Company commanded by Captain Braithwaite, who had recovered from his injuries sustained in the drop, led the advance and were in turn led by Lieutenant Thomas's Platoon. Thomas had also recovered from his wounds and recently returned to the fold.

The hedgerow selected for the line in advance was the long side of a narrow rectangular field of about fifty yards width and two hundred yards length. As Thomas's Platoon were moving forward up the line of the hedgerow it was just beginning to get light and the Commanders of the rear companies were, very rightly, hustling their men over the railway line as this was likely to become a most unhealthy area."

A machine gun opened up somewhere in front on the leading troops just as they reached the far end of the hedge and Sergeant Fay was killed and Lieutenant Thomas seriously wounded. The advance was checked, but the hustling over the railway line was continued in the rear and as a result practically the whole of the three rifle companies were, in due course, along the line of the same hedgerow. The specialist Platoons and the bulk of HQ Company had been left behind to rejoin in daylight at the objective.

"It was a most unhappy position for the Battalion to be in, especially as it was getting lighter every minute and serious opposition and counter attacks could be expected. The 12th Battalion had had some difficulty over their advance and were only just beginning to cross the railway line at the time. Thomas's Platoon was held up. It would be at least thirty minutes before they could launch their attack on the village."

Pine-Coffin's first move was obviously to cover the open flank, so a section was dispatched to search the corresponding long hedge on the right of the rectangular field. Having searched they were to remain there and see that no Germans got into it. In the meantime 'B' Company endeavoured to locate the gun that had fired on them and the other two companies had no alternative but to remain along the hedgerow where they had been halted.

"Things started to happen almost immediately and they happened on both flanks simultaneously. The section which had gone off to search the hedge on the right completely surprised a small German detachment with a very business-like dual-purpose gun mounted on wheels and in position on the hedge itself. It is an unpleasant thought to visualise what this gun could have done to the Battalion had its crew been more alert. It was in position and already pointed in the right direction and not more than fifty yards away. Practically at the same moment as this bit of luck on the right all three companies in the hedge position reported troops in the extended order advancing across the next field to them. They were coming straight for them and did not seem to know what was in front of them.

This was presumably the 13th Battalion coming up and orders were issued at once that there was to be no firing. As they got closer it was possible to see, in the half light, that they included amongst them a certain number of Germans, but that these Germans were not being made to move with their hands up and it appeared that some of them even had weapons too. This was a very odd way to bring prisoners in and was very unlike the 13th Battalion so a very close watch was kept on the whole party.

At about fifty yards it was clear that it wasn't the 13th Battalion at all, but a party of Germans about a company in strength advancing to the attack. The unfortunate position in which the Battalion found themselves was instantly converted by pure luck into one of unprecedented advantage. The best part of three rifle companies were lining the hedgerow with a good bullet proof bank in front of them and were completely screened from view to the enemy. The Germans came on steadily like living targets moving up the range and quite obviously had no idea what was in front of them. It was a dream target, almost too good to believe, but at the same time too much like murder to be seized at once. I decided to try and capture the lot alive. A Bren gun was moved out to a flank with the double object of covering the Germans and preventing them from working a similar threat on the Battalion's own flank. Lieutenant Mills was posted to a suitable spot and ordered to hail the Germans when they were 25 yards from the hedge and order them to lay down their arms. When he first shouted to them the consternation amongst the Germans was amusing to watch. They were taken completely by surprise and much pointing and gesticulation took place amongst them. They were in a very nasty position, but did not know just how nasty it really was. Some of them started to argue, but a few had the sense to lie down, when they would have at least presented a slightly harder target. This absurd situation lasted perhaps thirty seconds when it was ended by one of the Germans who did a very stupid thing. This man lay down and opened fire on the hedgerow with a machine gun. 'A' Company, the centre one, was at once given the order to open fire and great execution resulted. The firing was kept to a minimum and a Platoon of 'C' Company under Lieutenant Archdale was sent out from the left of the hedge to bring in the Germans as prisoners. Within fifteen minutes the German Company, as it proved to have been, scarcely existed, the bulk of them were prisoners, a large number were dead and precisely three had managed to slip back in the morning mist to escape into the wood. One of these was captured a few days later.

The prisoners were sent back to Brigade HQ and the Battalion moved on and occupied its objective without further excitement."

The objective was not an interesting one at all as it only consisted of some ground on the flank of the village. The 12th Battalion were luckier as they had the village itself. Meanwhile the 13th Battalion began to pass through the position on their way to carry out the further part of the operation, which was to take the prominent feature known as Hill 13 which lay just beyond.

The Germans employed their usual tactics on this hill keeping the bulk of their force behind the top where they were just out of sight. The 13th had little difficulty in reaching the top of the hill, but were then themselves attacked immediately and resolutely by a strong force. This was also at the very moment when they were least prepared to receive it, being out of breath from the climb up the hill and disorganised after their assault. They were forced to fall back with considerable casualties to a position just in front of the 7th and to leave the Germans in possession of the hill for one more night. This was a serious set back because every hour gained by the Germans gave them that much more time to prepare their positions and made it that much harder to drive them out and put them on the run again.

The night was quiet and was spent in speculation as to whether it would be the 7th or the 12th which would make the next attack on the hill. Many thought that it might well be a combined attack by both Battalions and everyone realised that the longer the delay the harder the job would be. No patrolling was necessary by the Battalion during the night as the 13th Battalion were still between them and the enemy, so there was a good opportunity to make up for the sleep lost the previous night.

August 19th was a glorious day with a bright warm sun shining to make the men feel glad to be alive. **"It really was pleasant to lie around in the sun while the destruction of the enemy to the immediate front was being planned. When the orders were issued the spectators found that they were all wrong because they had over-**

The Tale of Two Bridges

looked the fact that the Division now had another Brigade on its strength. The Special Service Brigade [Commandos] had been fighting on its own line and one had almost forgotten that it was now part of the Division. General Gale had not forgotten though and he decided to use it for this job."

Throughout the day reconnaissance parties from this Brigade kept coming up and having a good look at the hill which they had been ordered to take, with a full Brigade attack, that night. The General had decided to use the whole Brigade in one attack to ensure that the hill was taken and that the Germans did not get another night's respite.

"The Germans put up a stiff fight as the hill was a commanding feature and very useful to them as long as they could hold onto it. However, the Commandos had them off it before daylight and were strong enough to beat off the inevitable counter attack on the top. The Commandos were then ordered to swing left handed and regain the road to Dozule, which they did successfully. The situation at 0800hrs on the 20th of August was therefore that the advance had got as far as Dozule, but there was still a stretch of road which had been by-passed during the attacks on Putot and Hill 13 and which would have to be cleared. There were known enemy at this strip of road and they were sufficient to prevent 3rd Brigade from being rushed to Dozule to continue the advance there, but they were insufficient to warrant the delay of deploying the Brigade for an attack, nor did such a plan of action suit General Gale. The Divisional Commander liked to push forward with one Brigade in the lead, but with another one following closely behind and keeping in touch so that he could slip it through and into the lead at the critical moment. In this way he was able to maintain the momentum of the advance and the enemy could be attacked continuously by day and night. The opposition on this strip of road was probably only slight, but it would be sufficient to delay the 3rd Brigade, which was still at Goustranville and would therefore have to attack frontally down the axis of the road.

The 7th, however, were nicely placed on the flank and so the job was given to the Battalion. Two simultaneous patrols were

The Tale of Two Bridges

sent out from the Battalion position; both of Platoon strength and both found from 'C' Company. The left hand one, under Lieutenant Archdale, was directed onto a large house at the Goustranville end of the strip and the other, under Lieutenant Pape, into a farmhouse at the Dozule end.

This little operation was carried out in daylight and turned out to be a model of its kind.

Archdale's party reached their objective with little difficulty and were in perfect wireless touch throughout with Battalion Headquarters, but some anxiety was felt for Pape's party as no answer could be got to the wireless messages which were sent to them and no messages were received from them. It was also clear that they had run into some opposition as there were sounds of small arms fire from the direction of the farmhouse. Archdale was ordered to send a small party laterally from his position with the object of contacting Pape's party. This party did not establish the desired contact, but reported that there was shooting in the area of the farmhouse and it was assumed that Pape was having to fight for it. It was not clear though why we had received no news and as the distance was short Major Woodman, the Company Commander, went off to join him with his batman as escort with another wireless set. It was possible that Pape's set had gone off net so this second one was carefully netted before starting off and Woodman kept in constant touch with the Battalion Headquarters as he moved out.

Woodman followed the course he had ordered for Pape to take and was surprised when he eventually came to the farmhouse without having seen anything of Pape or his Platoon. Here he was in something of a predicament himself as he had reached his objective without having achieved his own objective. Which had been to contact Pape and find out what was happening. He assumed that the patrol must have taken the house and that they were by then installed in it and the fields beyond, so he and his little party moved into one of the small out houses in the farmyard to see what they could find out. It soon became evident to him that he had come a bit too fast and also that Pape was elsewhere when he saw German soldiers moving about in the ground within a few feet of him. There was nothing to do but wait where he was and hope that none of them chose to come into his shed. Fortunately this little incident, which might well have been a tragedy, ended up on an almost comical note. While Woodman and his party were toying with the idea of shooting some of the Germans, Pape's patrol completed their preparations and launched their attack on the farmhouse from their new direction.

The assault was completely successful and several Germans were killed in the house, but the leading troops, flushed with success, were not a little surprised to find their Company Commander awaiting for them beyond their objective. This was the sort of thing one got on exercises, but it shouldn't be allowed to happen when one is doing the real thing.

The little operation opened up the road as desired and was only marred by one fatal casualty. Wilson, the lone sniper of the Bois de Bavent days, had been killed by a sniper during the initial advance of Pape's party. It was this little incident that had made Pape alter his original line and go at the farmhouse from another direction. His wireless set, as had been suspected, had gone off net soon after he started.

Later in the day (August 20th) the Battalion moved across and occupied the road strip itself. This proved a very welcome move because the house that Archdale's party had taken possessed a large garden, which was filled with beautiful fruit, just ripe for eating, while Pape's farmhouse turned out to be a cider storage plant containing vats of cider, stretching from floor to ceiling. A long stay would have been very welcome, but this was highly improbable as the 3rd Brigade had already passed through Dozule and the advance was on again at full speed."

The town of Pont l'Eveque lies astride the river but it is not bisected by it. The bulk of the town is on the near side. Here the bridge had not been blown, but the Germans had withdrawn across to the far side and were holding that side and the bridge itself.

On the morning of August 22nd the 13th Battalion was in the town on the near side of the river and was in contact with the enemy holding the bridge, while the 12th Battalion had also reached the river and were at a point about half a mile south of the town. Both Battalions were engaged in a shooting match with the Germans across the river and were trying to slip parties across at all possible crossing places. The 7th were on some high ground just to the rear of the 12th Battalion and were busy with their preparations to force a crossing of the river that night on the sector in front of the 12th Battalion as ordered.

These preparations included a number of visits to the 12th Battalion by Pine-Coffin and the Company Commanders to take advantage of the very good view which could be had of the far bank from the upstairs windows of a house which the 12th Battalion were using as an observation post. This house was in an ideal position and commanded an uninterrupted view of the river from its upper window. This fact alone made it a painfully obvious observation post and, as if this were not enough, the house itself was isolated. It must have been an even more obvious target than the church at Goustranville had been and it is difficult to know why the Germans did not shoot it down as they could so easily have done. It was visited by many senior officers, including the Divisional Commander, who would have been a very worthwhile target, but luckily it was not ever seriously engaged. The Frenchman who owned the house was very anxious to help.

"He had a very unfortunate habit of getting very excited and on more than one occasion this caused him to rush to the open window and point out some landmark or other with wide sweeps of his arms. As he was wearing a very light coloured shirt and no coat, his information soon became more welcome than his presence. General Gale, on one of his visits to the observation post, decided that it might be possible to bounce the enemy from his position by attacking at once instead of waiting until night. He issued the necessary orders and the 12th Battalion began their attempt."

The 12th Battalion made a very gallant try, but circumstances were against them and by evening it was clear that they would not succeed and the attempt was called off. Their effort and casualties had tired them considerably and there was a danger that the enemy might themselves cross the river and counter attack them during the night.

They were completely withdrawn for a rest and their sector was taken over by two companies of the 13th Battalion. This took place in the town and was aimed at crossing the river over the main bridge. Their attack met with a certain amount of success in the early stages and they succeeded in capturing the bridge, but ran into very stiff opposition in the built up area on the far side. They hammered away at it all day, but never really looked like breaking through the rest of the town and in the evening they were ordered to withdraw back over the bridge. It was originally intended that they should reform in their original position, but as this was being shelled as they withdrew and they already had considerable casualties they were pulled right back out of the town to a rest position in the rear. The remaining Company of the 7th was then ordered to take their place and hold the near side of the town.

"It was not an easy job to get this Company into its new position, as the decision to move was not made until fairly late, it was then a question of getting them in as soon as possible and not by any particular hour."

At the time this Company was just in the rear of what had been the sector of the 12th Battalion, but which was now occupied by the other two rifle companies of the 7th. All transport was, of course, further back in the rear. Fortunately Pine-Coffin was up with the 13th Battalion at the time the decision was made and was able to warn them over his wireless of the move, so that by the time he got back to them himself, they had almost completed a hot meal and a certain amount of wheeled transport had been gathered together.

There were two routes to the area: either by the direct route, which ran parallel to the river, or by a more involved one which used a lane further to the west. The direct route was naturally by far the shorter and it was not completely exposed to view as it was screened by a fairly thick hedge, although this had the usual number of open gateways. The only vehicles were jeeps and trailers, but it was found that if these were all loaded to capacity, with no regard for the springs, the whole Company could be moved in three trips. As time was of the greatest importance Pine-Coffin decided to risk the direct route and set off in his own jeep with the first party at a "cracking" pace.

The Tale of Two Bridges

"All went well until three quarters of the run had been completed, when a machine gun opened fire from the far bank of the river and wounded Private O'Sullivan who was in the trailer of the second jeep."

Pine-Coffin and the Company Commander, who were both in the leading jeep, got through successfully and were able to plan the dispositions of the Company when it eventually arrived. The rest of the little convoy had been halted by the machine gun incident and the passengers had to tumble out and finish the journey on foot through the back gardens of the houses. When they arrived in Pont l'Eveque they found that the reconnaissance had been completed and they were put into temporary covering positions which enabled the 13th to withdraw.

"While all this was going on the drivers of the jeeps were carrying out one of those fine bits of work which one came to expect from them as a matter of course. The soldier who fights on his feet is inclined to regard the jeep driver and, in fact, anyone whose job enables him to avoid marching, as one to be envied - a man with a soft job. It is not a simple job to turn a jeep with a trailer attached in the width of a narrow road at the best of times, but to do so when any movement is more than likely to attract a burst of machine gun fire is very tricky. Nevertheless, all the jeeps and trailers were got back safely to the start point and the rest of the Company were run up, without incident, by the alternative route."

The Brigade's position was unsatisfactory and even more so the Battalion's. Two Battalions were tired out and resting in the rear, while the 7th was extended across the whole Brigade front in what appeared to be a purely passive role. The Company in Pont l'Eveque itself seemed to have the best chance of getting forward again and so they were ordered to patrol vigorously at first light. The Germans had a habit of slipping away during the night and Pine-Coffin felt that they might do it here, so he was up with this Company himself very bright and early.

The patrol reported, as expected, that the enemy had gone. The town appeared to be free to enter. A platoon was sent to hold the far side of the bridge and a wireless message to the rest of the Battalion to be ready to move at short notice. It would take some time to get the Battalion collected together and on the move, but it would be too disheartening if another Battalion had been passed through to take the lead. Fortunately the Brigade Commander paid an early visit to the area himself and when he heard the patrol report he ordered the advance to continue. The 7th were allowed to lead as they were by then all standing by and ready. Various objectives were laid down and christened with their own code names for easy reference as they were reached.

In order to save time the Company in the town was ordered to search the buildings for snipers, but to be ready to join the rest of the Battalion as it passed through. They found no snipers at all and when the rest of the Battalion entered the town they were ready to move with them.

The main problem was one of how to get forward with speed. The enemy were not in the town and it was not possible to know for certain when they had left and whether in fact they had left on foot or in vehicles.

"It was unlikely that any of the civilians would know for certain and anyway they were all so excited that it was difficult to get anything out of them at all. Whether the enemy had gone by vehicle or not, it was quite clear that the Battalion would have to follow on foot, because not only was the main bridge in the town now blown, but also another smaller one just on the outside of the town. Both of these fallen bridges were effective obstacles to wheeled vehicles and would remain so for some hours at least."

A touch of comedy was introduced by the excited inhabitants of the town who came out in great force and seemed anxious to fete the Battalion as their liberators. They produced bottles of wine and much excited information about the Boche and appeared keen to make a party of it.

"Many of the younger ones were mounted on bicycles of that flashy and rather sporting type so popular in France. With their dropped handlebars and narrow tyres they seemed built for speed and just the job for chasing the Germans. Ten of them were com-

The Tale of Two Bridges

mandeered with the object of mounting one section who could move well in front of the marching troops and, with luck, contact the enemy. There was considerable delay in getting this party on the move because it was decided that the cycles could not just be taken, but must be commandeered correctly with the usual exchange of signatures. This meant much laborious writing out of forms (in duplicate) so that the rest of the Battalion, on their feet, had made good distance to the east by the time the fast moving cycle section got going.

There was much amusement and wisecracking as they pedalled past the column, especially when it was noticed that there were only seven of them at this stage. The road was long and straight and two more came to grief before they were out of sight and the other five also finished the journey on foot."

The cycles were a good idea, but they were much too light for operational use and proved quite unable to stand up to the weight or strain. No opposition was met and it looked at one time as if the Battalion would reach its last objective without making contact at all. After some eight miles or so they came to a railway bridge over the road which had been blown completely thus blocking it. The scouts who crossed the debris were fired on from the woods on the far side and it seemed that this might be the scene of the enemy's next stand. It was a good position from his point of view and about the right distance from the last one.

'A' Company, which was commanded at the time by Captain Rogers, was sent off to occupy a small hamlet in a commanding position to the left flank and to carry out a flanking attack from that position. The actual order to carry this out was never given though because when General Gale arrived at the fallen bridge he decided to pass another Brigade through. The Battalion was ordered to secure a limited objective just beyond the fallen railway bridge, so as to give a good start to the Brigade being passed through. This little action was carried out successfully and quickly by 'B' Company, but not without some casualties which inclued Lieutenant Nicholls, who had only just

Capt John Rogers

got out to the Battalion from England. He had arrived four days previously and was seeing his first action.

The day of August 25th was spent very pleasantly in the area of Saint Andre d'Herbertot and everyone would have relished a lengthy stay in that very pretty little place. However, this was not to be as that same evening Pine-Coffin was summoned to Brigade HQ and given orders for the advance, which was to be pressed the next day with the Brigade in the lead.

The speed was to be hotted up from now on and plans were in hand to use lorries to carry the troops. The lorries though could not be produced out of thin air and in the meantime the advance would continue on foot as before. The Battalion was selected to lead the Brigade and this was a fine compliment to their marching qualities, but would impose great strain on them. They had already covered a very long distance on their feet and in addition had lost many hours of valuable sleep since the advance had started. It was now realised that they were not in the best of condition for a long fast march through the heat of the day. It was not known where the opposition would be met so the orders could only be to push on eastwards at best speed along the axis of the road to Pont Audemer, to get as far as possible along this road in the shortest possible time.

"The head of the Battalion was to pass through Beauzeville at 7am on the next day (26th). The condition of the Battalion's feet had not been improved by the static two months in the bridgehead and now caused concern."

Under the circumstances Pine-Coffin was compelled to inform the Brigadier that if opposition was not met before Pont Audemer itself, which was 22 miles distant, he expected to have to let some men fall out on the way because of their sore feet and, in some cases, because of their boots.

The Brigadier told Pine-Coffin that he fully recognised this possibility, but it was important to get on and the main object was to close with the enemy again in the shortest possible time and with the maximum number of men. He appreciated the difficulties of the Battalion, but relied on them to do their best and he would arrange for ambulances to follow up and collect those who had been allowed to fall out.

The march that followed these orders was one of the finest feats of the Battalion and will long be remembered with pride by those who took part in it.

"The advanced guard Company passed through Beauzeville exactly at 7am with the rest of the Battalion about a mile behind them. Everyone seemed to realise that much was expected of them and they swung along at light infantry pace. The road, for the most part, was flat and straight which meant that an apparently endless stretch of it always extended in front and as the sun got up later in the morning conditions rapidly became uncomfortable. The ordinary rules of march discipline were rigidly enforced from the start, but even so more and more could be seen limping badly as time went by."

Pine-Coffin was with his men every inch of the way. "It was found that the old army rule that pipe-smokers could continue to smoke on the move was not generally known and many of them got fresh comfort from their old favourites when this welcome news was passed around. Those who did not smoke at all or who only smoked cigarettes (which are only permitted to be smoked at halts) were able to share in the two other forms of encouragement which helped the Battalion on its way. Brigadier Poett was a frequent visitor and usually timed his jeep visits to coincide with one of the hourly ten-minute halts so that he could talk to the men as they rested by the side of the road. He made it quite clear to them on these occasions that he thought that they were doing splendidly, and the fact that he was taking an interest in them and was pleased with what they were doing undoubtedly helped those with particularly sore feet, and there were plenty of those, to keep going."

Other encouragement came from the inhabitants of the villages. Many villages were passed through and in these practically every civilian turned out and lined the street, cheering and giving flowers to the passing troops. Some of the more practical ones gave fresh fruit instead of flowers while some of them armed themselves with jugs of hot milk and piles of cups. The latter of which were the most popular of all and were a great relief to many a thirsty throat.

As the different stages were passed it became increasingly clear that little opposition was likely before Pont Audemer itself and that the march would be more a test of endurance than anything else. This it certainly was and more and more were limping and many were showing blood through their boots, but still the pace was maintained both by those at the front, who checked every mile against the watch, and by those at the rear who ensured that the column did not straggle.

"The distance between the twelfth and sixteenth mile was probably the worst of the lot and during this stage there was no singing or whistling and very little conversation. Just sheer foot slogging and at an uncomfortable fast pace at that. After the sixteenth mile the country became a little less monotonous and a new spirit seemed to animate the Battalion. The singers started off again and so did the whistlers. The whole column became like a runner who has just got his second wind. The pace was increased slightly to take advantage of this change and when a check was made about two miles south of Pont Audemer the column was found to have been marching faster than it had been at the start, furthermore it was still complete as not a single man had even asked for permission to fall out. The Brigadier came forward here and again expressed his admiration of the feat that had been achieved, but pointed out that he expected opposition in the town and that as the Battalion must obviously be tired he proposed to pass through another Battalion which had been brought up in lorries. When I pointed out that this would be a great disappointment to the 7th, he changed his plan and ordered the Battalion to continue in the lead and to occupy Pont Audemer."

It would have added further zest for this operation had it been known at the time that to enter Pont Audemer at all was to poach on the territory of another Division. The 49th Infantry Division commanded by Major General Barker, CB, CBE, DSO, MC, had the town on its line of advance, but at the time the Airborne Division was slightly ahead. General Gale's decision to take the town when he had the opportunity was obviously the course best suited to the prosecution of the war, but it was also a decision that could lead to an exchange of sharp words between the two Generals, as indeed it later did. **"This possibility was much appreciated at the time."**

The Tale of Two Bridges

The town of Pont Audemer is bisected by the river like so many towns in France. It was expected that the enemy would have withdrawn to the far side of the river and that they probably would have blown the bridges. This was in fact what had happened.

The far side of the town was the higher of the two and from positions on that side the enemy fired machine guns down the streets on the near side and put over mortar bombs and shells on likely places. It did not take long to confirm that the town on the near side of the river was clear of the enemy and this was accordingly occupied by the Battalion. However, during this process a few casualties were sustained from the machine guns on the far side and from the mortar bombs and shells.

The leading troops of the 49th Division reached the town the same evening (26th) and at the same time Generals Gale and Barker had their meeting on the subject, which would have been very interesting to listen to. It was arranged that the 56th Brigade (or 49th Division) should cross the river and clear the rest of the town on the following night and that the Battalion should remain where they were until this attack had succeeded. The Battalion was to come under the command of 56th Brigade for the action. In the meantime, on the night of the 26th, the 6th Airborne Division had completed its task and were withdrawn except for the Battalion.

The action of the 56th Brigade was carried out successfully as planned. On the following morning (August 28th) the Battalion was withdrawn from Pont Audemer and rejoined the rest of the Division with which it sailed for England, from the famous Mulberry Harbour at Arromanches, on September 4th.

Having now shared in the experiences of war and its consequences for the men of the famous 6th Airborne Division and of the 7th Parachute Battalion in particular, what can be said of their involvement and of the vital task of being charged with the responsibility for the successful capturing and holding of the two bridges over the Caen Canal and the Orne river? The calculated risks taken by the airborne troops in this engagement by storming a fortified bridge proved successful. Despite all the planning, these brave men had to take the risk and

The Tale of Two Bridges

advance over a bridge which they knew had been prepared with explosives, relying on the element of surprise to achieve their objective. Perhaps the following paragraph says it all.

After Normandy many new volunteers joined the Battalion. Which then took part in the Ardennes campaign and then 'Operation Varsity'.

The real tale of two bridges is the comparison of the success of Pegasus Bridge, as it is now known, and the later battle for the bridge at Neustadt which crossed the River Leine.

Here the 7th Battalion had lost the element of surprise and during their advance towards Neustadt the bridge was blown from under their feet, but that is another story…

The bridge at Neustadt … another story

Photo: Airborne Forces Museum

Chapter Nine

More Anecdotes

The following pages contain more anecdotes from some of the men still living who served with 7 Para. Some parts of these are in the main body of the previous pages, but many are not. By reading these full accounts a clearer picture of their struggles to re-group and of their adventures emerges.

Nick Archdale, written 25th February 2004:

"On the morning of 7th June I was on the Ranville-Breville road, dug in with the remainder of the 3-inch mortar Platoon, without 3-inch mortars but with one or two 2-inch mortars.

To my surprise I suddenly realised that there were quite a lot of German soldiers advancing through the wheat across the plain from Breville.

I decided to wait until they were close enough, when we started lobbing 2-inch mortar bombs behind them and shooting when they got up to run. It was great fun (an awful thing to say now), but I well remember Sgt. Freddie Fricker shouting to me to get down because there was a lot of return fire. In the middle of it all Col. P-C arrived to see what was going on, got hold of a rifle and started having a go himself. There were lots of shouts of 'I got one', but you could not be sure.

Soon after our drop in Germany several of us were sitting on the ground near a flat farm cart with a lot of very unpleasant air burst shell fire. As usual Col. P-C paid no attention to that and was in the middle of giving out orders when he was hit by a shell splinter that went through his face. His only reaction was to spit out a mouthful of blood and bits and carry on with his orders. Just before, we had been coolly discussing the merits of the special boots he had had made with straps instead of laces.

Very soon after that we were ordered to withdraw from our position and I believe this was the only time the 7th gave ground on any of our operations.

The Tale of Two Bridges

Later that day, in the evening, things had quietened down and I was sitting on the edge of my slit trench with my pistol in my hand. The troops crossing the Rhine had not yet reached us.

Suddenly I was grabbed round the neck from behind and I turned and very nearly shot my assailant, but luckily saw the face of my old friend Dwain Bramall who had come up with his 60th Rifles Company to relieve us. He subsequently became a Field Marshal and Chief of General Staff.

I believe the great thing about the 7th Bn. was that it was almost like a club of friends. Our Senior NCOs were a wonderful collection. There was never any shouting or bullying in the Battalion, but our discipline was second to none. We were never 'tough', but I really believe we must have gone to Normandy as one of the best units in the army.

Colonel Barlow was the perfect man to build the Battalion up and Colonel Pine-Coffin the perfect man to take us into action. I have always believed that I was wonderfully well blessed to spend the first four or five years of my grown-up life with such exceptional commanding officers and such wonderful fellow officers and men of the battalion.

When Colonel Tom Pearson took over in Palestine our luck continued. I was Adjutant in my last year, which was not much fun as all the old hands were leaving, but Tom was a great man to work for and has always remained a friend."

The Tale of Two Bridges

This next account is by E. Trueman and W. French who were dropped in the same plane as Archdale.

"The Battalion had started taking off from Fairford aerodrome sometime around nine o'clock in the evening, 5th June.

We were jumping from four-engined Stirling Bombers. Although the Stirling was an aperture jump, it was perhaps the most comfortable of this type of exit. Quite roomy in the fuselage, if my memory serves me correctly, carrying twenty-three parachutists. Once the doors were unhinged and clamped the 'hole' was quite immense. If one had stood seven feet tall it would have been virtually impossible to 'ring the bell', a stupid term dating back to the old Whitley 'jump' when one pushed too hard from the edge of the hole and crashed ones face painfully on the opposite side.

W. French

E. Trueman

Our particular plane was numbered 151 and named 'The Yorkshire Rose'. I had spoken to the navigator before emplaning and, armed with the prior knowledge that our flight path would take us some way down the Avon Valley, I asked him how close we would be to Bradford on Avon, my home town. After consulting his charts he said we would veer before the town, but if it was possible for me to plug into the intercom he would come through when the plane banked somewhere over Limpley Stoke. Which he very kindly did.

Strangely enough the one thing which remains very clear in my memory concerning the flight over England and the sea is the fact that I managed to smoke a whole packet of ten 'Joy Sticks'. For the uninformed these were cigarettes nine inches in length. Quite a feat. If performed these days it would probably merit a mention in the Guinness Book of Records.

Immediately upon crossing the French coast just prior to the order, 'Stand up, hook up, sound off, equipment check', one of the lads, Perry to be exact, who happened to be plugged into the intercom, remembers vividly the following conversation: 'Rear Gunner to

Skipper, better throw her about a bit, there's a bandit on our tail.' Meaning, of course, that an enemy fighter was close upon us. 'Skipper to rear, Wilco.' The pilot certainly reacted and threw the huge bomber about the sky like a toy balloon. The sad thing though, as we know now, that the enemy fighter had dropped back and shot down the following Stirling which was carrying nineteen of our friends, ten Vickers medium machine gunners and nine 3-inch mortar men. This 'plane crashed at Douvres Le Déliverande, where its occupants are buried in one long line - nineteen Paras and six aircrew.

Shortly afterwards - red light, green light and we were away. Again strangely enough, to this day I have no recollection of the actual drop, neither do I recall the impression of the ground appearing to be rushing up to meet me. Nevertheless I do remember hitting the deck, probably the worst landing I have ever made, shook every bone in my body. Then the real problem, I could not turn the quick release on my chute, obviously as a result of tattered nerves and sheer fear. I remember distinctly drawing my fighting knife, stupidly thinking in my panic-stricken condition that I could cut my rigging lines and thus free myself. Eventually common sense prevailed and I calmly stuck the knife in the ground, turned and struck the quick release and I was free. I remember thinking - what the hell am I doing here, this is stupid. Other than the sound of receding aeroplane engines and the explosions of bursting bombs a few miles away it was strangely quiet. I took stock of my surroundings and came to the conclusion that I had no idea whatsoever where I was. Everything on the maps and land models had seemed so easy and clear. The tower of Ranville Church, separate from the main building. The RV at the bottom of the village. But standing where I was nothing was familiar. The other remarkable thing which suddenly struck me was that I was entirely alone, not another living thing visible, not even an animal.

Our Vickers machine guns had been dropped in containers from the Stirling bomb bays. The principle was that they would float down on their chutes, land upright on their base, which would in turn activate a flashing bulb on the top of the container. Wonderful idea in theory, but search as I might I could not see any flashing lights. In actual fact we never did find our guns. It was days before we were eventually provided with new guns from Britain.

I had been on the ground for half an hour or more. Where the blazes was everyone? Six Battalions had dropped in at once, some three thousand or more fighting men - it was an impossible situation. Then through the gloom and haze, perhaps a handful of yards away, a figure approaching - Friend or Foe? I could feel the hairs on the back of my neck beginning to prickle. Sten gun in hand, 0.32 automatic in the other, I nudge towards the mystery figure. Then as if by mutual agreement, at perhaps thirty yards distance from each other, we give the age old order, 'Who goes there?' We ran towards each other. He shouted, 'Thank God Eric' and me shouting, 'Thank God, Bill French.' I recall how we threw our arms around each other, both probably shedding an emotional tear.

At this very moment from a distant hedge to our left a machine gun opened up. We threw ourselves to the ground and watched the tracer hurtling above us and disappearing into the distance. Fortunately, after a five-second burst, the firing suddenly stopped and once again quietness reigned.

Now the inquest - Where the hell are we, where are the others, particularly the remainder of our 'stick'? As if to answer our question, three more figures suddenly appeared, these were from our planeload. Eventually, after a further half an hour or so, our group had swelled to twelve. Twelve from the original 'stick' of twenty-two. It has never been satisfactorily explained to me what actually happened to the remaining ten, except that several of them were captured immediately upon landing. The experts can only conjecture that a freak wind gust somehow or other caught the other members of our planeload and blew them off course

Luckily Sergeant Bill French was an excellent map reader and all in all a splendid fellow to have around in an emergency. It was obvious to us which way the coast lay, the explosions and smoke was proof of this fact. I recall how we were lying in a sunken lane when suddenly, during a lull in the explosions, in the far distance came the faint crackle of small arms fire. Frenchie uttered, 'Well lads at least we now know in which direction to head.' So, like all good soldiers, led by Sgt. French, we started to double towards the sound of battle. Sufficient to say that, after doubling for some four miles, we emerged on to the solid roadway some hundred yards from the bridge over the River Orne.

The Tale of Two Bridges

Dozens of stories have been written over the past forty odd years dealing with the fighting and the holding of the two bridges, there is very little that I can add to these accounts, except for me to say that I didn't find it very funny. The sight of the 7th Bn (LI) The Parachute Reg. and to 'D' Cy. The 2nd Bn The Ox. and Bucks. Light Infantry, when Lord Lovat and his Commandos eventually got through, had to be seen to be appreciated. The Green Berets mingling with the Red ones was a sight which again can only be explained by those men who were actually there.

I remember throwing my arms around a huge Scottish Commando, his very first words, 'Well you can go home now, Cherry Beret, the real men are here.' I must admit that I would have given anything to have complied with his statement."

My Memories of Meetings and Sightings

The above title refers to the occasions that L/Cpl R.B. Follett met or saw his Commanding Officer, Pine-Coffin, during their service in the 7th Battalion (LI).

"Lt. Col. Pine-Coffin was a professional soldier who had seen active service with a Para Battalion in the North African Campaign, during which time he was awarded the MC.

L/Cpl Follett

L/Cpl Follett was a 'civilian in battle dress' who applied himself to the vigorous and concentrated training and discipline needed to the best of his ability.

I served in the Army for 4 years and 7 months. August 1942 saw me join a training Battalion of the Royal Scots at Berwick on Tweed. (10th ITC).

Ten months later I was at Bulford Camp having volunteered to become, I use a 1943 word, a 'Paratroop'.

The Tale of Two Bridges

Gordon Barracks, Bulford, was the home of 7 Battalion (LI) The Parachute Regiment, the unit to which I was drafted, together with drafts from other Regiments, to join with the former members of 10th Battalion, Somerset LI.

This was the Battalion that made the arrangements for our Battle Course training at the Airborne Forces Depot, Hardwick Hall, Derbyshire and for parachute training at RAF Manchester, Ringway.

I am pleased to say that in July 1943 I returned to the Battalion at Gordon Barracks complete with a Red Beret with a green diamond and a Winged Badge which, among other things, qualified me to meet the Commanding Officer of the 7th Bn (LI) on several occasions and it is these that I intend to relate.

The first meeting was the day that Lt. Col. R.G. Pine-Coffin, DSO, became my Commanding Officer and addressed and welcomed me, and the rest of the Battalion of course, as we paraded on the square of Gordon Barracks. It was also my first attempt at Light Infantry drill!

I noticed that his voice was positive as he told us what he expected of us and recall his final words. For in a quieter tone than previously he said that, 'Training will commence as of now, as we prepare to face the Hun.'

The second meeting was our briefing at Tilshead Camp, Salisbury Plain in mid/late May 1944, when again in a very positive voice he assured us that the hard work we had put into our training would stand us in good stead, 'Because we are heading for Normandy, France, and the 7th Battalion can be proud it has been given the plum job of two bridges over the Orne Canal.'

I was wounded on June 6th 1944, having got no further than Bénouville."

A Worm's Eye View, Edward (Teddy) Poole

Lt Poole

"Towards the end of 1940 a school friend and I, being fed up with our public school, which incidentally had a strong military side, planned to join the Army. He had a strong advantage, his father was a Lieutenant General and Baronet, something that still counted in those days.

I walked down Whitehall having decided to join the Brigade of Guards. However the portly Recruiting Sergeant standing on the doorsteps took one look at me, decided that I was not Guardsman material and told me that the Guards were not recruiting that day. He suggested that I tried a Recruiting Office at Hendon. At Hendon, I passed the medical and was sworn in with about five other recruits. We were each given a small advance of pay (more than the King's shilling) and a railway warrant to our various destinations. My destination was a 'Young Soldiers' Battalion of the Middlesex Regiment stationed in the Grand Stands at Hurst Park Race Course. The race course no longer exists.

Once we were out of hearing of the Recruiting Officer, the bulky red-sashed Recruiting Sergeant called us together, 'Usually,' he said, 'I march you young fellows down to the station and on the way we call at the pub and you buy me some beer so that I can drink to your health and success in your Army career. Unfortunately today I am too busy and so I'll take the beer money now.' He held out his hand. We paid up. We were too green to object.

I had attended a boarding school from the age of seven and so I was well prepared for Army life. Arriving at Hurst Park I reported to the Guardroom, situated in a wooden shed surmounted by a frame which signalled the race winners. The Sergeant of the Guard sat at a brown blanket-covered table covered in coffee-coloured returns, drinking tea. At the back of the Guardroom three prisoners with shaven heads were scrubbing the floor under the supervision of a Regimental Policeman. The prisoners advised me to, 'F*** off while there's still time.'

The Tale of Two Bridges

Just before 'lights out' was sounded that night I undressed into my pyjamas. This caused a sensation amongst my fellow recruits in the barrack room, one of the bars of a grandstand. A number of them got out of their beds to inspect me. The majority of my companions shed their battle dress and boots and slept in their issue long johns, vest and socks.

The following day, together with other recruits, I was issued with my battle dress, SMLE rifle, First World War webbing and greasy ammunition boots. We were then given inoculations which caused us diarrhoea, for which malady the grandstands were ill equipped. We were given 24 hours to get over the problem, during which time we were busy with button sticks, blanco and trying to get a high polish on the toe caps of our new, greasy boots.

At this time the Army was extremely short of instructors owing to its rapid expansion. I had been in the OTC at school and had passed my 'Cert A' and so I knew something of drill, weapon training and map reading. I was soon promoted, if promotion you can call it, to the role of acting, unpaid, Lance Corporal. I had to demonstrate drill movements and weapon training for the Sergeant Instructors, turn out recruits properly dressed for their parades, oversee that the barrack room was clean and tidy and, about every ten days, act as Second-in-Command to the Sergeant of the Guard.

Twice a week the junior NCOs were called out for further training after the normal parade hours by the RSM. He would pick on us for imaginary faults such as a speck of dust on a rifle, dubbed as 'indescribable filth'. He would then offer to report us to the Company Commander 'for sloppy turn out' or as an alternative we could have a toe to toe boxing match with him in his office. The RSM had been a welterweight boxing champion, but age and the Sergeant's Mess beer had slowed him up. I had boxed at school, I was six foot three and weighed over fourteen stone, I could out reach him easily. I managed to land a few stinging blows one day, after which he picked on men of his own size.

During the London Blitz, the Battalion was sent to Purfleet, Thames-side, Firing Ranges.

We were housed in Nissen huts and slept, as at Hurst Park, on palliasses spread on bed boards. One night a German aircraft unloaded its incendiary bombs over the marshes and the camp. We evacuated our huts, but unfortunately a bomb had hit one Private in my hut, as he lay asleep on his bed board. He was killed instantly.

I was promoted to full Corporal and even received the pay of my rank. One day I was marched in front of the Colonel who asked if I would like to be put forward for a commission. I said yes. Luckily for me the psychological and initiative tests for potential officers had not been initiated. I was called for an interview at Leaconfield House. I think the three-man board was chaired by a Brigadier assisted by a Major and a Captain. I was asked a few questions about my school. 'You must know X's son.' I did. 'Do you play rugger?' 'Yes, I was in the fifteen and was secretary of the Boat Club.' I passed. I was due to go to the Black Button OCTU at Petrim Down, but I was knocked down by a learner riding a motor cycle, broke a leg and was taken into hospital.

When I was discharged from hospital, I was sent to a rehabilitation camp situated in Richmond Park in order to regain fitness. I was most anxious to be discharged from the camp to be posted for my officer training. By luck this happened quite quickly. For some reason I was approaching a wired compound behind the cookhouse. A civilian van was being loaded somewhat surreptitiously with food from the cook house and with coal. I reported this to my Company Commander and was posted back to my unit the next day.

Back with the Middlesex, now in cavalry barracks at Hounslow, I was sent for a medical to ensure that I was still category 'A1', before my posting to an OCTU. I was embarrassed to find that the Medical Officer was a young lady for whom I had to strip. She examined my leg, inspected me below the belt while I coughed. She passed me as A1.

As any other rank, I had volunteered without success, whenever a call had appeared on Company or Battalion Orders for strong swimmers, the Commandos or for Parachute training. My Commanding Officer, who was to be posted to the Airborne Division, had told me that if I passed out in the first three places at OCTU, I might be considered for parachute training. At that time most volunteers were more senior officers who usually dropped rank on joining.

The Tale of Two Bridges

I was posted to an OCTU at Barmouth in North Wales. The wild countryside leading up to Snowdon to the north and Cader Idris to the south of the Mawdach estuary was ideal for our tough exercises.

An early incident gave my Company a good laugh for which we paid. We all wore that abomination of headgear, a sidecap, on which badges were difficult to see. On our first morning the Company was drawn up on the square at the seafront. The RSM Johnny Copp from the Coldstream marched onto the parade, pace stick under his arm. He started to question us. 'You there,' he shouted in that extraordinary voice that was issued to RSMs together with their warrants, 'What were you before you came here?' 'I was a Sergeant, Sir.' 'Well you were a sloppy idle Sergeant in a sloppy idle Regiment. What was your Regiment?' 'Coldstream Guards, Sir.' Copp's face turned a few degrees more purple and we were doubled around the square with our rifles at the slope and then down to the soft sand of the beach. I escaped being shouted at for 'Idle lacing of boots.' 'You know where to go,' (the guard room). 'Quick march!' Whereupon the miscreant was doubled off the parade by two Drill Sergeants. Sometimes the RSM would halt as he passed between the ranks. 'Am I standing on your hair?' This was said to a cadet whose hair was almost as long as a gooseberry's.

One of the few relaxations was attending Military Law and Officers Mess etiquette lectures, given by a charming old Colonel who had served in the Boer War. Like naughty school boys, we only had to mention General Buller and law and etiquette were forgotten and Buller's career was expounded. Sometimes he would intervene with a 'Salty' story which would terminate with a man and a girl 'doing that most wonderful thing'. Something that we young men were most anxious to achieve.

The father of a friend I had made at the OCTU was a General who had served in The Royal Irish Fusiliers. I was invited to dine with him at the RAG. My behaviour must have passed muster and I was commissioned in his Regiment. The Fusiliers, although charming, were understandably annoyed when they discovered that I was using them as a stepping stone towards becoming a parachutist, and I was loaned

The Tale of Two Bridges

to a Battalion of The Ulster Rifles. Luckily I knew riflemen's drill, as my school OTC had been 'black button'.

Soon I was called for an interview at the 7th (LI) Parachute Battalion which was forming at Bulford. Walking up to the mess I was amused to see a mobile canteen with a brass plaque announcing that it had been presented to the Airborne Forces by the Butlers and Footmen of Long Island.

The Battalion was based on parachute volunteers from the Somerset Light Infantry and took volunteers from all Rifle and Light Infantry Regiments. It was commanded at that time by Lt. Col. Hilary Barlow. I came under the wing of Tommy Farr who was Platoon Commander of No. 4. Platoon, 'B' Company, under Major Roger Neale. I managed to behave correctly and was accepted, subject to passing my parachute training.

A few weeks later I was posted to the 7th. I expect the hospitable Ulsters were glad to see the back of me and I dreaded the thought of not passing my parachute training and being RTU'd. At Bulford I was issued with a red beret, but of course as yet no parachute wings. I was posted to 'B' Company to command 5 Platoon and taken on the strength on May 1st 1943.

Soon I was despatched to the Regimental Depot in the grounds of Hardwick Hall, where the parachute courses were put through very hard fitness training and some preliminary parachute ground training. A few members of my course were not fit enough and were RTU'd. Eleven officers and 88 ORs were sent to Ringway on course No. 65 on May 17th 1943. Here the RAF instructed us in how to land with the correct roll, how to kick out of twists in our rigging lines while in the air and how to exit the aircraft, which at the time was a Whitley. This plane carried ten parachutists seated 5 on each side of a small hole. We could carry only our automatics and Stens when jumping. Our packs, Bren guns and other heavy equipment were dropped in containers in the middle of the stick.

Before our first jump from a balloon we undertook a test of nerve. We climbed a ladder into the roof structure of a high hangar. One by one we donned a harness attached to a wire which was wrapped round a small drum equipped with small fan blades. We then launched ourselves onto a gym mat below. The unwinding drum was braked slightly by the fan blades. One or two could not face the test and were RTU'd. Then we were taken to the dropping zone at Tatton Park to watch the previous course jumping from an aircraft. It was not a jolly introduction to our future profession. The next day we did our first jump from the basket of a balloon. During the days that followed we did five jumps from a Whitley and one more daytime jump and one night jump from a balloon.

All 11 officers and 72 of the initial 88 ORs completed the course. I returned to Bulford, but was not yet allowed to put up my much desired parachute wings until I had made a jump with the 7th Battalion. At last the time came. We took off from Thruxton in Whitleys for a Battalion night exercise. I was then granted a week's leave and qualified for two shillings a day parachute pay.

During the succeeding months of hard training around Bulford, as a Second Lieutenant I was delegated fairly often to supervise the volunteers' preliminary test of covering fifty miles across country within 24 hours, carrying full kit and weapons. I was sent on a number of courses including street fighting in a bombed out area of Battersea, a sniper's course in a pleasant Devonshire seaside resort and a battle school. This was not at the airborne battle school in Derbyshire, but at an infantry school situated in the New Forest. We were expected by Colonel Hilary to be at the top of the list at the end of these courses. The other students at the battle school were determined to beat the wearer of the 'flash' red beret and the instructors were equally determined to show me up.

One night at battle school we were all taken by sealed lorries and dropped off, one at a time, some miles from the rendezvous. We were on our honour not to use roads or railway lines to help our return to an RV. The Demonstration Platoon were sent out to capture us. This was an exercise that I had performed many times and so, when I arrived at the RV well in advance of the other infantry men, the Commanding Officer of the school preferred to think that I had cheated.

At about four in the morning, when all but a couple of students had arrived at the RV, the Colonel ordered everyone to embuss 'except for Lieutenant Poole, who can find his own way back'.

The Tale of Two Bridges

The lorries drew out and the Colonel, having waited a few minutes for the laggards to appear, jumped into his Humber staff car. Without being seen in the dark, I managed to wedge my boots onto the back bumper and cling to the large cleated spare tyre. The Mess was only about five miles down the road in a requisitioned private house surrounded by rhododendrons. As the car turned into the drive I dropped off the bumper and ran up to the front door of the mess just as the Colonel was entering. I panted as if I was out of breath. I was prepared to say, if questioned, that I had followed his order to 'find my own way back'. The Colonel said nothing and I was afraid that I might get a bad report. However it transpired that he had a sense of humour and all was well.

In January 1944 Lt. Col. Barlow was awarded the OBE in the New Year's Honours List. He was to be promoted shortly and posted to the 1st Airborne Division, to be Second-in-Command of the 2nd Airlanding Brigade. One of our Company Commanders, Major Wallis, was posted also to the 1st Division as Second-in-Command of the 2nd Parachute Battalion. Unfortunately both were killed at Arnhem.

By now the parachutists had been given bigger and better aircraft. Roomy Stirling bombers which were unpopular with bombing crews because of their lack of ceiling, but ideal for us with their big aperture which allowed twenty parachutists to exit the plane carrying heavy equipment in a bag attached to a leg. A quick release, after the parachute had opened, allowed the bag to be lowered on a cord to the ground first. We also jumped from smaller Albermarles and from side doors of Douglas C47s.

A 5th Parachute Brigade was formed under Brigadier Poett. To our temporary annoyance we were moved to this Brigade and replaced in the 3rd Brigade by the newly-arrived Canadian Parachute Battalion with whom we soon became friends. They were forgiven. Our new Commanding Officer was Geoffrey Pine-Coffin, who had commanded a parachute battalion and had been decorated in North Africa.

During January 1944 the Battalion commenced mobilisation and continued intensive divisional exercises during which we had several

The Tale of Two Bridges

fatal casualties and major and minor injuries. In April Major Steele-Baume joined as Second-in-Command of the 7th. During April the Battalion won Divisional Rugby Championships. I played at wing forward in the days when wings got away with being slightly offside.

It was in May 1944 that the 6th Airborne Division paraded on the Dropping Zone to be inspected by the King and Queen.

Marching at ease back to Bulford a loud voice in 'A' Company was heard to say, 'Who was that smasher walking behind the Queen?' Colonel Geoffrey answered, 'She was a Lady-in-Waiting.' Voice from 'A' Company, 'If I was King she wouldn't be waiting long.'

May 1944, 6th Airborne Division inspected by The King and Queen

Map: Airborne Forces Museum

General Montgomery, about whom many of us had certain reservations, also arrived to inspect the Division. After the inspection all officers from Lt. to Major General were paraded in the Bulford Camp Theatre for a talk by Montgomery. After General Montgomery had left for his car our popular Divisional Commander, Major General Richard Nelson Gale, climbed onto the stage and announced, 'I know what you all think, you think he is a s**t, well he is but a very efficient one.'

At about the end of April or beginning of May the Battalion camped out in the woods between Exeter and Exmouth where we practised river crossing with inflatable rubber dinghies on the Exe and its parallel canal. Of course we did not know at this period the reason for our exercise. The locals were told that we were having a rest from our hard training. To back this up, we had a good deal of time off.

Towards the end of May 1944 we moved to a sealed camp at Tilshead, not too far from Fairford aerodrome. There on May 27th all officers were briefed by the Colonel, helped by excellent air photographs and a wonderful model of the area and our objectives for June 5th. My only criticism was that, in contrast to the excellent UK Ordinance maps with which we had trained, the maps of France were of poor quality. Once we had moved out of the briefing area, they became a mild handicap. We now realised why we had practised river crossing on the Exe. It was in case of the failure of the gliderborne coup-de-main party of the 52nd, whom we of the 7th were to relieve. To take and hold the bridges over the Orne and Caen Canal intact, before they could be blown up by the Germans.

Early in the morning of June 6th, I jumped at No. 1 from a Stirling aircraft. Strangely enough I had always felt slightly apprehensive when jumping on exercises, but on this occasion I had so much to remember from my briefing that I was not nervous. Perhaps because of my size, in addition to my heavy operational load I carried an inflatable 'J' Class rubber dinghy in my leg bag. As I descended I was lucky enough to see, outlined by the light of an explosion, the unmistakable church tower of Ranville, which stands apart from the main building. As a result I had no difficulty in identifying the whereabouts of the Battalion RV. I was lucky enough also that the majority of my Platoon found their way fairly quickly to the RV.

At the RV we heard Major Howard's signal that his gallant coup-de-main had been successful. The inaccurate drops had slowed the arrival at the RV of many of the Battalion. My Platoon had been lucky and it was nearly up to strength. Lt. Col. Pine-Coffin changed its orig-

The Tale of Two Bridges

inal task and ordered us to occupy the village of Le Port, which stood over the bridges on the road towards the beaches. It was vital to reinforce the 52nd as soon as possible. The advanced Battalion HQ set off, crossing the canal bridge at 0140hrs.

During our advance on the village we heard a German group behind a hedgerow we were about to cross. I tossed a 36 grenade over the hedge. After the explosion we heard the sound of running feet and cries of a wounded German soldier. At dawn we were troubled by snipers from the church tower. I tried to rush the tower with a small patrol, but we were driven back down the narrow staircase by stick grenades and Schmeisser fire. The tower snipers were eliminated later by an accurate shot from a PIAT. Major Howard and his coup-de-main party came under the command of Col. Pine-Coffin at about 0210hrs. By 0325 all objectives were occupied and held against various counter attacks.

The bombardment of coastal positions by naval guns and rockets, prior to the seaborne landings at 'H' was impressive. Smoke and dust rose to a great height which could be judged only by the sight of the supporting fighters, which looked like model planes against the dark cloud of dust and smoke.

I cannot remember the exact timing on the evening of D-Day when we saw the welcome sight of gliders of the Air Landing Brigade, swooping down to their landing zones. As well as the gliderborne infantry, the gliders contained the Divisional RA with some 17-pounder and 6-pounder anti-tank guns and their lightweight field guns and the Divisional Reconnaissance Squadron.

General Gale sent a special signal to GOC 3rd Division to urge relief for the Battalion; the hand over was completed at 0015 on June 7th. I remember snatching a few minutes' nap on some flea-infested straw in a barn before re-crossing the bridges. Then the Battalion went into Brigade reserve at Le Hom.

We were busy digging our slit trenches, encouraged by being mortared and shelled. I was handicapped at this time by a severe back pain which, together with my heavy operational load, made me move like a crab. I was worried that I would be evacuated back to the UK, but luckily my back cured itself during the time we were in these trenches.

The Tale of Two Bridges

We were re-supplied by air drop. I remember thinking that the 14-man ration packs in three varieties, although very welcome, had been designed by a humourist in the Quartermaster's department, as it proved impossible to distribute the rations fairly. The contents as I remember included, in addition to tinned food, such luxuries as 2 sheets of WC paper per man, some cigarettes and boiled sweets.

The Battalion took up position on the edge of some woods near Breville. From our trenches we could lean out and pick wild strawberries, it was the first time I had tasted this delicious fruit. We were in reserve during the bloody battle for Breville and we were unimpressed by a few infantry men from a well publicised regiment which had been sent up to reinforce the 6th Airborne for the attack, who ran back on a track in the woods past my Platoon position.

Rain poured down and an order went out for an issue of rum.

On the 18th a large fighting patrol was organised to attack the farmhouse. The Brigadier wanted gunners to shoot up the area before the patrol attacked. I suggested a silent approach but I was over-ruled. When we attacked the enemy were already alerted. My Platoon was on the left flank. At the last moment as we lined up to charge we saw a previously concealed enemy machine gun post on our flank, near a crossed track. I took my runner, we managed to silence the machine gunners. I gambled that the German field gunners were ranged on another area. I was wrong. There was a loud groaning noise like a giant rusty hinged door being opened as the rockets of a multi-barrel mortar fired. We were both severely hit by the fragments.

My runner was killed and I was on the ground with my left foot at an odd angle while a fragment of metal penetrated my right hip and passed through that leg and into the other. Some of our chaps some how got me back to Battalion HQ at enormous risk to themselves."

Edward Poole, MC

The Tale of Two Bridges

Sergeant Fred Fricker, from Colford, Somerset, wrote (for home consumption) in 1944 from a rest area some three weeks after the capture of the bridges:

"Those days of preparation were hard - often 6 days without sleep and often 24 hours without a scrap of food or water, continually flying and parachuting - but they surely hardened us for the event which will play a big part in the liberation of Europe.

Sgt Fred Fricker

I well remember all the final preparations we made so that nothing should be left to go wrong. I must have checked my mortar containers about 5 times before they were loaded on to the Stirling which brought 20 men and myself into 'the midst of mine enemies: Goodness and mercy has followed me' through, up to now. Thank God!

I remember we gave all our English money to people as we were on our way to the 'drome, keeping our French money just in case we needed it. The Air Force (good chaps) gave us a hearty send off and took most of us safely to our destination. The journey was 'cushy' until we arrived over the shores of Normandy and then ack-ack opened up at us. Some planes were hit: we were hit but not seriously. Our pilot and crew flew us to the area where we were to drop, near those 2 notable bridges, which have now been named 'Pegasus Bridge' and 'Light Infantry Bridge': both are now holding Airborne signs.

No one knows except those who've experienced it what it is like to be in charge of a plane holding 20 other brave men who are about to jump into the jaws of the unknown. No, I wouldn't say unknown, for we certainly knew more about Jerry than he expected;

"INTO A REALM OF UNCERTAINTY"
by
Paratroop Sergt. Fred Fricker.

SOUVENIR
COLEFORD COMFORTS WEEK 1944

but a jump into a realm of uncertainty. Nothing was certain. We could have failed. Thank God we didn't.

There we were in a little world of our own and my job was to make sure that my men left the plane before it turned on its way to England again. You can't imagine it of me, but I even had my pistol close at hand. Just in case one man should not want to jump with us. One man 'jibbing' could cost the lives of the rest of the crew. But I had no trouble. My men were as hard (even harder) than ever I was.

I'll never forget following my last man out into the inky black morning about 1am. We were not anxious about our parachutes opening: no, there was plenty of fun going on around us before we even touched down. Many of our chaps never reached the ground alive. Those who did were soon engaged by enemy troops. Many of us were dropped at least two miles off the spot intended. The Air Force were gallant and brave men to fly through such enemy ack-ack as we came up against. Many had to turn to avoid being blasted to pieces. Yes, they were brave crews who took us over to Normandy. Many did not get back to England.

I remember touching down in the middle of an orchard about 2 miles from my Bn's RV to find an ack-ack gun in the corner of the field or orchard and an MG 42 was firing tracers just over my head into my chute. I lay low in the long grass and allowed by chute to blow away from me, leaving me where I had landed. The MG 42 continued to fire at the chute and must have taken it for granted he had 'bagged one more'. He may even have been making one more Swastika sign on his butt when I crawled - as I've never crawled before - away to the nearest hedgerow.

My job now was to find my containers for my mortars; but I felt I must go carefully as in the drop I'd lost my Sten gun and all my equipment except my pistol which I'd tucked into my clothing. I never found our containers. Nobody did, for the plane I had left had 'caught a packet' as I jumped. I did not know then of course, for there was firing and roaring of planes everywhere around. All the planes were ours. I thank God for leaving me with my pistol, for in it were 7 rounds, and by the time I had found another Englishman the Boche was 2 men down.

After what seemed ages I met 2 men and, after ensuring that they had come in one of the planes flying overhead, we made plans to get to the bridges. This part of Normandy is very close and wooded; in fact like a jungle in places and so we were lucky to find a man who could speak French. Calling at the first house we found the frightened French people gave use the information we required, but asked us to leave them quickly. They probably thought it was another 'hit and run' raid.

Very soon I had about 30 men who were lost from various Regiments. With this little force of men we soon got to a larger body of men, acquiring weapons on the way. After dumping the majority at Bn RV I took my own men and we arrived at the bridges just in time to hold it against the Boche. What actually happened was that about 180 men in 6 gliders landed right slap beside the bridges just as we were to attack. Our Bn was only about 50% strength, yet the bridges were taken without losing a man: surprise had played its vital part. But as soon as the Boche knew what had happened he attacked; but somehow God was on our side and we held out. It was a tougher fight than had been anticipated.

The joke about the drop was that we landed slap on a Boche Regiment that was on a cycling scheme. All my men soon had Jerry bicycles!

The bridges were now ours, but could we hold out against these attacks against MG 42 and 34s, shells and mortars until noon? It was now about 2am. These were the thoughts that flashed through my mind as I saw 1 man then 2, 3 and 4 men sniped and killed right beside me.

Daylight came and up to then I didn't even know if the opposite bridge was still in our hands; but now I could see our airborne men fighting a gallant battle against untold odds. Tanks came with daylight, but our PEATs behaved wonderfully and I saw at least a dozen tanks turn and run after our boys had stopped eight. An armoured boat came up the canal, but it never went back for our PEATs took a pat at it. The crew gave themselves up. About 7am we made a push: it was successful and on our bridge we gained a piece of high ground and almost the whole of the village. Here we fought and dug. We had plenty of ammo and our grenades were useful for Jerry came in very close to us, expecting us to surrender.

Many French women braved the whizzing bullets to give us cider and drink. They were very grateful to us. I saw one of my men kill a sniper who had just sniped our RSM's batman. The French people had *seen it too and before he could do anything to protect himself he was being kissed from all angles by women and men.*

We held on till noon, the time we were to be relieved; but no-one came. Then we heard the sound of bagpipes in the distance. A Scottish Regiment of Commandos had come through from the beaches to help us out. Next came tanks and more troops. We expected to be relieved and sent back to the beaches, but within 24 hours of landing we were launching another attack. We fought in this part which is like a jungle against an enemy who is cunning too, for 20 days and nights without a relief.

We have often been attacked, but each time my little Platoon of mortars has played a big part in holding Jerry off. On one recent attack we didn't get it all our own way; my 15 men and 3 NCOs fired 1,300 mortar bombs during the attack which lasted for three solid hours. Jerry doesn't like our mortars and he finally broke loose and pulled out, fully disorganised. His shells and bombs, too, are deadly. He often makes life very unpleasant and I remember one night when he shelled us continually for two hours. We were still able to drive him off afterwards.

We have been resting several days now and no one seems to know what's to be done next. I do know that this Caen area has Jerry armoured divisions spaced 3 miles apart. The normal distance is about 20 miles apart. So each yard of ground has to be bought very dearly.

We've had good food, plenty of sweets, chocolate and cigarettes, and our mail has been coming through quite well. We have just started getting 1 slice of bread per man per day. English bread is good after living on hard biscuits for about five weeks.

I do hope I haven't been boring, for to me these last few weeks since D-Day seem a lifetime. I consider myself lucky to be alive to write, for out of 43 men in my Platoon we now have 19. There were 5 of us Sergeants when we started: now there's only me.

Thank you all for what you have done for me. God controls the destiny of men. One day I hope to be amongst you again, proud to be a Colsfordian!

God Bless you All."

Sgt. Fricker was seriously wounded in Pont Audemer in August 1944, but survived the war

Grangues, Ernest Mold (Medic)
[qualified as a doctor after the war]

"At the briefing we were told that Section 2 of 225 Field Ambulance, under Captain Wagstaffe, was to be attached to the 7th Battalion and would set up a forward RAP in Bénouville in support of 'A' Company.

The section was (wisely, as it turned out) split into 2: Captain Wagstaffe took half in one plane; the rest, including George Jamieson and myself, embarked on another whose number on the airfield was - if memory holds - 164.

We experienced heavy flak over the coast; the plane was certainly hit but not, I think, significantly; green light came on seconds later. George Jamieson jumped at No. 4; I followed at No. 5. I remember a great deal of tracer as we dropped. George and I landed within sight of each other in a fairly small field. The only thing that was clear was that we were not on the DZ. We were in wooded country on the upper slopes of the hill. In fact, as we worked out later, we were just above the village of Grangues a very short distance to the NE of the German HQ.

We went downhill, through a gate and met up with two more members of our section. In the orchard beyond we nearly ran into a party of perhaps 50 Germans; we escaped detection by flattening ourselves against the trees. We next avoided a sentry, then ran into and extricated ourselves from a picketed mule train. We saw, down the hill, anti-parachute posts being hastily erected.

Next, a glider under tow came into view; the towing cable was released and we watched it coming in to land. Suddenly it turned towards us; George leapt one way and I the other; it passed between us, tearing off its wing and turning over as it crashed. We thought no-one could have survived, but to our amazement all the glider men piled out, Sten guns at the ready. We gave the password - very hastily - and joined up with them. The Sergeant agreed with our already-formed guess that we should head SW; we proceeded very cautiously and slowly. We ran into a German patrol who either did not see us or decided that discretion was the better part of valour.

Soon after dawn we found ourselves at the foot of a little hill; we climbed up far enough to get a sighting view and saw below us the flooded valley of the Dives. I had a map and could identify our position without much trouble. A brief council of war; the Sergeant reckoned to lay up 'til dark; George and I thought that was inadvisable and, by agreement, set off on our own, planning a route by map. The two RAMC Privates followed us at a short distance. We came to a road, hiding behind the hedge while a column of tanks rolled by, then crossing it to the cover of the other hedge. By chance there was a milestone - Dozule 3km - which confirmed our position. Beyond us lay open country with a farmhouse about a quarter of a mile away. We felt it wiser to crawl along a ditch (filled with brambles) and by-pass it.

The other two, following us, were held up at the road by more tanks; then, more trustful than we were, they made for the 'friendly' farmhouse - where they were promptly captured by the German occupants. This I know from one of them - Private Troutt - whom I saw a few years ago. He had no idea of what became of his companion, from whom he was separated in the prison camp.

We, meanwhile, passed through farmlands with adequate cover. We heard the Navy's bombardment at dawn - here we saw the results; field after field of dead and mutilated cattle. We came to the disused railway line a short distance from Putot-en-Auge station. Here, by another chance, we met a French woman with a child; she told us there was a machine gun post at the station. We had already located a sentry a few yards in the other direction. We seemed trapped; there was no cover at all beyond. So we decided to walk across the open ground, openly, and without hurry, relying on being unidentified in our (German-like) helmets and camouflage smocks. In fact we crossed the space and reached a minor road unchallenged; we paused in a convenient copse. Then a great surprise; we heard the familiar sound of army boots; we peered through our cover and saw a group of unarmed and dispirited Germans closely followed by fully armed British paratroopers - from, I think, the 9th Battalion.

This handful - eight or nine men - had been dropped astray, as we had been, but had managed to wreak havoc on their way back, shooting up staff cars and even the German NAAFI at Troarn. We joined them gladly. The plan was to avoid the Dives floodings and cross the river lower down, perhaps at Bures. On the way we picked up a

The Tale of Two Bridges

couple of British airmen who had been shot down; they were quite unhurt and cheerful.

Then, in a wood on the outskirts of Bassenville, we came upon a crashed glider (taking heavy equipment and a jeep) with its pilot and co-pilot. One of them had a broken leg. It was now late in the day (June 6th) and it seemed a good place to rest up. As it grew dark a movement in the bushes revealed a group of sinister-looking men in dark clothes and berets - French Resistance fighters, the Maquis. They brought a sack of Bren gun ammunition and a cask of cider. It was a very good evening, though we kept quiet on account of the stream of tanks passing on the road just beyond the wood. The French left, eventually, taking the prisoners with them; no-one enquired what would become of them.

In the morning I stayed back in the wood with the wounded pilot (we had splinted his leg and made him as comfortable as we could) while George went with the rest of the party and a guide from the French men on reconnaissance. They came back after some hours, having decided that the best crossing of the Dives was by the - by then destroyed - railway bridge at Bures. They had received a scribbled message that a number of wounded Canadians were concealed in the Chateau de Bassenville.

We manhandled the jeep out of the glider; one of the party drove George, myself and the wounded man to the chateau, while the rest of the party set off independently.

At the chateau we were very well received with a hastily cooked breakfast and a liberal allowance of Calvados. Then George stayed with the wounded, in the barn, while I went in the jeep as far over the marshes as it would take me and then on foot to the bridge. I crossed the wreckage of it successfully and then there was nothing left to do except to saunter quietly through the Bois de Bavent until I saw a red beret - though there were still a few obstacles to overcome before, at about 5 o'clock in the evening (June 7th), I rejoined the Field Ambulance at the Bas de Ranville. That night a patrol from 9th Battalion led, I believe, by Colonel Pearson himself, with jeep, rubber dinghies and a requisitioned horse and cart, brought George and all the wounded back from Bassenville."

Grangues Memorial

This report is compiled by J.S. Shinner, passenger in EF 295, A.E. Price, rear gunner in EF 295, J. Porter (brother of S.C. Porter, Telegraphist, RN)

"Few people have heard of the tiny village of Grangues, 5km south of the town of Houlgate in Normandy. It was never the scene of a major action yet it was here that, on the night of June 5th-6th 1944, fifty soldiers, sailors and airmen lost their lives.

Almost certainly the reason for this is that from the air the River Dives looks remarkably like the River Orne and Grangues could be mistaken for Ranville. Facing problems due to flak and patchy cloud, a number of the invasion aircraft mistakenly headed for Grangues. Matters were not made easier by the fact that the area is hilly; in fact the grounds of Grangues Chateau lie along a ridge which is 100m higher than the intended dropping and landing zone at Ranville.

Two Stirling paratroop carriers, among several from 620 Squadron RAF, had an uneventful trip from their base at Fairford. However, crossing the French coast they encountered accurate AA Fire. EJ 116, carrying men of the 7 Parachute Regiment and of the Reconnaissance Corps, must have been severely damaged. It crashed at Grangues, exploding on impact; there were no survivors. EF 295 carried 15 men of 591 Parachute Squadron RE including the OC and two from HQRE. It, too, was hit as it crossed the coast and one or both port engines caught fire. At the same time one or more of the explosive 'sausages' being carried by the sappers for the clearance of the landing zones was ignited and started a major fire inside the aircraft. Four men jumped immediately, but the remainder could not reach the exit hole and stayed in the aircraft until it crashed. Some of the paratroops were killed in the crash, but there were also some survivors.

The chateau was occupied by a Company from the 711th German Division and survivors were soon rounded up. When the gliders came in later in the night at least four of them made the same navigational mistake. Two crashed in the grounds of the chateau. One carrying Divisional HQ personnel hitting trees and finishing up vertically nose down. Another landed just across a road and a fourth about a mile away.

The Tale of Two Bridges

At some time during the night the survivors from EF 295, with the exception of two badly injured men and one officer, who was removed for interrogation, were among eight soldiers who were executed by the Germans."

An appeal was made for a memorial; the chosen site is within the confines of the Grangues churchyard. It is a granite slab topped with a bronze Pegasus; the bronze plaque has three columns of 17 names in each.

Rank	Name	Arm/Service/Unit	Aircraft	Remarks
F/Sgt	Atkins E.H.F.	RNZAF	EF 295	
P/O	Barton A.H	RAF	EJ116	
Lieut	Belcher R.C.	Recce Corps 6	EJ 116	
F/Sgt	Bittiner H.M.	RAF	EJ 116	
L/Cpl	Branston K.W.	591 Para Sqn RE	EF 295	
Lieu	Bromley J.L.	Glider Pilot Regt	Horsa	
Pte	Copson G.	7th Bn Para Regt	EJ 116	
Sgt	Crosse G.	RAF	EJ 116	
L/Cpl	Davies S.A.	Military Police	Horsa	(Probably Div HQ)
Tpr	Done M.P.	Recce Corps	EJ 116	
Cpl	Earwicker P.T.	Recce Corps	EJ 116	
Spr	Evans J.J.	591 Para Sqn RE	EF 295	
Pte	Francis R.A.E.	7th Bn Para Regt	EJ 116	
L/Cpl	Fraser T.A.	591 Para Sqn RE	EF 295	
Pte	Frost V.P.C.	7th Bn Para Regt	EJ 116	
L/Cpl	Gascoigne J.	7th Bn Para Regt	EJ 116	
Spr	Guard P.	HQRE	EF 295	
Cfm	Hunt	REME	EJ 116	
Capt	Hunter R.A.	RA	Horsa	(FOB Group)
CSM	Hutchings J.E.P.	7th Bn Para Regt	EJ 116	
Cpl	Kelly W.A.	591 Para Sqn RE	EF 295	
Cpl	Kemp A.R.	7th Bn Para Regt	EJ 116	
Tpr	Lamont G.W.	Recce Corps	EJ 116	
Cpl	Leamer G.H.	7th Bn Para Regt	EJ 116	
S/Sgt	Luff R.A.	Glider Pilot Regt	Horsa	
Tel	Martin A.F.	Royal Navy	Horsa	(FOB Group)
Sgt	Maund G.	RAF	EF 295	
Capt	Max J.H.	AAC	Horsa	(Div HQ)
L/Cpl	Mitchell R.L.	7th Bn Para Regt	EJ 116	
Sqn Ldr	Pettit W.R.	RCAF	EF 295	
Pte	Piper W.P.	RASC	Horsa	(Div HQ)
Tel	Porter S.C.	Royal Navy	Horsa	(FOB Group)

The Tale of Two Bridges

Rank	Name	Arm/Service/Unit	Aircraft	Remarks
Sgt	Powell B.	Glider Pilot Regt	Horsa	
L/Cpl	Reardon Parker J.	591 Para Sqn RE	EF 295	
Sgt	Reid D.	RAF	EJ 116	
Pte	Scott W.	7 Para Bn Regt	EJ 116	
Pte	Shutt	7 Para Bn Regt	EJ 116	
Sgt	Smith J.G.	RAF	EJ 116	
Pte	Stobbart R.W.	7 Para Bn Regt	EJ 116	
Dvr	Thompson G.	591 Para Sqn RE	EF 295	
L/Cpl	Twist R.	7 Para Bn Regt	EJ 116	
Cpl	Van Rynen A.	7 Para Bn Regt	EJ 116	
Sgt	Wallis W.E.	RAF	EJ 116	
F/O	Watkins R.G.	RAF	EF 295	
Spr	Wheeler D.H.	591 Para Sqn RE	EF 295	
Tpr	Wilson A.H.	Recce Corps	EJ 116	
L/Cpl	Winfield W.	RUR	Horsa	(Div HQ, Def, Pl)
Spr	Wolfe F.	591 Para Sqn RE	EF 295	
S/Sgt	Wright D.F.	Glider Pilot Regt	Horsa	
Spr	Youell J.	591 Para Sqn RE	EF 295	

The text is as follows:

...the Allied Expeditionary Force landed on the Normandy beaches to launch an assault upon German occupied Europe. To protect the eastern flank of the invasion against counter attack, the British 6th Airborne Division had the vital task of taking and defending an area east of the Orne River in the hours preceding the beach landings. Taking part in this advance operation, in the very early hours of 6th June, two Stirling paratroop transport aircraft with men of the Parachute Regiment, the Reconnaissance Regiment and the Royal Engineers were shot down close to the Grangues Chateau near here. Soon after, two Horsa gliders with Divisional Headquarters personnel and a Forward Observation Party (for the Naval Bombardment) also crashed within the Chateau grounds. Forty-three soldiers and airmen died or were mortally wounded in these crashes and eight survivors, who had been made prisoners of war, were later shot in the Chateau woods. These young men were all volunteers whose belief in the cause of freedom was such that they were prepared to give their lives in this dangerous mission. Let this peaceful place preserve a lasting memory of their names.

>The text is then repeated in French.

Diary of Gordon Brennan - MTSec
Spring 1943 to Fall 1952

"*After my parachute training at Hardwick Hall and Ringway, where I earned my Para Wings, I joined the 7th (Light Infantry) Battalion of the Parachute Regiment in the spring of 1943 and was placed in 9 Platoon, C Company for a start and then into MT Section as a driver/dispatch rider, but I still had to participate in all the training routines beside driving/riding when required, so didn't have much time to think about upcoming operations, only time to bless the powers that be when we went on a night march or some crazy scheme, or to attend a mine-clearing lecture or a course on how to dig a regulation slit trench, though I must admit all were later to be put to good use and, of course, there were more training jumps. I always remember one in particular on 13th December 1943 from Hurn Aerodrome using Fleet Air Arm Albemarle's. The DZ was at Netheravon and we were the lead aircraft. The jump was cancelled because of high winds, but somehow the message never got through to our pilot and we jumped from our aircraft and when we landed we were dragged at a good rate of knots until we had control of our 'chutes. Unfortunately one man was dragged into a stone wall and was killed.*

Prior to D-Day we went into a concentration camp where we were wired in and no one without a special pass was allowed out, here we made sure that all our equipment and arms were in top shape, especially our fighting knives, which we all had concealed in a pocket in our Battle Dress slacks. I did manage to get out once. I was detailed to take the Assistant Adjutant, Lieutenant Richard Todd (later a famous film star), to Oxford to pick up the sand table map showing the area we were to jump into. The following day we were all shown the sand table model which was a very exact three-dimensional model of the terrain we were going to land on and were briefed on the exact jobs we were each expected to do when we arrived.

On the afternoon of 5th June we marched to a small field, had our evening meal, which was brought to us a little early, and then the Padre held a short service of dedication and the Colonel addressed us, stressing how important our job was. Then we were loaded onto trucks and driven to Fairford aerodrome where we fitted on our equipment and 'chutes. I personally, a young man of 19 years weighing at 150 lbs, tipped the scale at near 300 lbs with all my gear and parachute on; thank goodness we only carried one 'chute, unlike our American counterparts who jumped with a reserve. The second 'chute would not have been any use anyway because we dropped below 500 feet and there would not have been time enough to use it. Also at the airfield we were given tea and light snacks to eat whilst we were waiting around and then we boarded the aircraft, with a little help climbing in because of all the equipment we were carrying. Once we were airborne we started singing all the old war songs from, 'Pity the Poor Parachutist' to 'Roll Out the Barrel'. In a fairly short time we received the order to stand up and check each others' parachute hook up and equipment. Looking out we were able to see all the fireworks - anti-aircraft tracer shells - being fired at us. Then it was red light on - green light - and Go! and out we went, each with his little clicker to identify friend or foe.

We didn't have much time to orient ourselves on the way down, just a quick glance at the departing aircraft and then bump onto the ground, with machine gun fire all around. Our rendezvous was to one side of the DZ and the Colonel had a hunting horn, which we had heard on numerous occasions in the past, so off I went, using my clicker when I encountered anyone in the dark. When I reached the rendezvous and the Colonel had gathered enough men there we all set off at the double down the escarpment to the bridges which had already been secured by Major Howard and his detachment of Ox & Bucks Light Infantry and Sappers. We then crossed over the bridges into Bénouville and deployed all around the village, meeting resistance and eliminating it as we went. Snipers were a problem for a while, particularly from the church at Le Port until Cpl Killeen took out the belfry with a PIAT anti-tank round; there we found twelve dead German riflemen. We were moved around a bit to meet any German counter attacks as they developed, then shortly after

The Tale of Two Bridges

noon we heard the sound of the pipes of the Commandos led by Brigadier the Lord Lovat who marched through our lines as cool as a cucumber and led his men across the bridges to his own objectives.

At times two or three of us had to help with the stretcher cases from near the Chateaux. At some time during the day Jerry broke into the village and shot up our RAP (Regimental Aid Post), killing wounded on stretchers, medical orderlies and the Padre. And then rush back to our positions where it was give and take all afternoon until about 2100hrs when the Glider-borne Brigade came in, most of it landing behind us, on our former DZ, but the rest of the Ox & Bucks Battalion landed to our front, which they cleared of any sign of immediate attack, giving us a short respite, and then crossed over the bridges re-absorbing Major Howard's Company. Just before midnight we received the word that we were being relieved by one of the seaborne infantry battalions, the Royal Warwick's I believe, and at midnight I was able to make my way back to the bridge. I think of the original 660 men there were maybe 200 of us able to walk away.

Once across both bridges we dug our little hole in the ground and got a few hours' sleep, the following morning we marched up the escarpment to a small orchard by Ranville where we dug in and sort of regrouped. The weather was not very favourable, but didn't bother us too much, then, after we had been there a couple of days, a Spitfire with its cockpit cover open circled us and when we waved the pilot waved back at us, then he took a wide swing round and came back with all his guns blazing, fortunately no-one was hit. We heard later it may have been a captured Spitfire piloted by a German.

Motorcycle packed for dropping; and ready for use

The following day I asked if I could go back to the DZ and see if I could find the 125cc James motorcycle that had been dropped for my use, so Jack Chambers and I went and searched among the gliders and containers and luckily found the motorcycle. We also found a jeep that needed a

The Tale of Two Bridges

little fixing, also one that had been hit by a shell; we were able to cannibalize this and get the other jeep running so the Bn now had a transport section again. We loaded the m/cycle onto the jeep and then we spotted a German half track near the place where the Royal Marine Commandos were. I asked around and was told that they had been unable to start it, but I did and drove it back to our unit thinking it would save the machine gunners and mortar men from having to carry such heavy loads. Very well received by them, but in a little while the CO sent for me and said that the Marines were not happy to see what they regarded as their prize disappear down the road. They had spoken to the General about this and it had come down the line that it was to be returned, so I was instructed to take it back, which I did.

 I had just returned when we were told that we were going to attack and take a wooded area that had a German unit in it. We were detailed off with the sub-machine gunners slightly in front of the grenade throwers and when the sub-machine gunners had let fly they were to drop to the ground and the grenade throwers were to lob their grenades into the enemy position so we cleared the woods. The following day we moved up the ridge into a farm building and we immediately came under fairly heavy fire and had a tough time holding onto the position. Six Sherman tanks came up behind us to take the pressure off us, but unfortunately they were all soon damaged and put out of action. Next the Black Watch from the 51st Highland Division attacked through us, making far too much noise for our liking, but assuring us that things would soon be taken care of. Anyway, at daylight the attack went in and they received a severe mauling. Next day another 51st HD unit came and relieved us and we moved to the village of Hérouvillette where we dug in around the village and were mortared and shelled frequently. At one point the CO sent for me and said he could not get through on the radio and I was to take a message to Bde HQ that German tanks were massing at a given map reference and I was to deliver the message to the Brigadier personally. On the way to Bde HQ I was subjected to a fairly intensive mortaring - I guess my little two stroke m/cycle made too much noise. On the way back, because of the mortaring, I crashed into the ditch and the m/cycle was destroyed. As I made my way back on foot I came across a German BMW m/cycle with a wrecked sidecar attached to it, so the following day I went back with Jack Chambers, we removed the sidecar and rescued the m/cycle, once again bringing the transport section up to full strength. I asked for and received an authorisation from no less than 7 Corps HQ to use the German machine (this certificate from 7 Corps HQ is now in the Regimental Museum).

Whilst we were in Hérouvillette we were able to sample good French bread and Camembert cheese; these tasted so good after days on Bully Beef and hard Cheddar cheese and hard tack biscuits, and we were able to brew a good cup of tea. Generally it was not too bad here, occasional mortaring and shelling and we fought off a few attacks. One time there was a farm house across some open fields from us and a German tank would poke its nose around the corner and take a few pot shots at us and then pull back. Well we came across a damaged 17-pounder anti-tank gun, with just one wheel missing, so that night we hauled it into position, blocked up where the missing wheel should have been and then trained it on the corner of the farm house. When the tank next put its nose round the corner we had a good surprise for it. We got our shot off first and one shot did the job, one dead Jerry tank. After about a week we were instructed to move up the ridge again past the brickworks and then a few miles into the Bois de Bavent, a thickly wooded forest with small clearings with farms on them dotted here and there. Here we relieved the 8th Battalion for a rest and this was to be our home for several weeks.

Because of the constant shelling and mortaring we dug deep and scrounged doors and timbers and roofed our slit trenches in, not only making them safer from overhead shell bursts which rained shrapnel down, but also made them a bit more comfortable to live in. At first we took a few casualties, but then we got used to the mortars and listened for the 'pop' when they were being fired, also there were the 'Moaning Minnies', 6-barrelled rocket mortars which made an awful screeching sound as they came over, making it feel like they were heading directly at one, whereas in fact they probably landed hundreds of yards away, but other than that they were not too effective - a loud bang and that was it.

There was an occupied farm (we named 'Bob's Farm'), in front of us on the left flank and we tried on several occasions to take it, but failed, and this only served to aggravate the enemy which meant more shelling and, of course, we had more wounded. Then came the rains and it didn't seem to stop and we were in trenches knee-deep in water and sometimes deeper. I had extra duties being the dispatch rider and I was detailed nightly to take the day's situation report to Bde HQ. Jerry must have had directional listening posts because he tried to mortar the road. Some nights I would go faster and try and outrun them and at other times I would flip a fast 'U'-turn and run back, anyway I'm here to tell the tale which always means a happy ending. When I got back the Capt Quartermaster always poured me out a double tot of rum. People I remember being taken away wounded at this period were Joe Westby, Pat Reason, a young fellow from Yorkshire, Pat Pearson and John Butler.

The routine was pretty well set by this time, stand to one hour before first light and until one hour after, that is unless we were going to put in an attack such as on Bob's Farm, which we did again and this time lost one of our officers, a Scottish chap, his batman tried to help him but to no avail. The farm was too well fortified and Jerry too well dug in around it. Back to routine: on a normal day we would then get breakfast sent up, often tea and porridge and sometimes fried bacon, from the ration packs, all chased down with hard tack biscuits and margarine and jam and cheese, of which there always seemed to be plenty about, then we would clean our weapons and check ammo and grenades and then try to get a little sleep for which we would take turns with our partner in the same slit trench We fed well on what were called 14-men packs, these had canned rations for 14 men for one day or 14 days for one man. These were brought up daily by rear echelon trucks along with the ammo and any other supplies we might need. The packs had seven different varieties so that in theory we could have different meals each day for seven days, but it very rarely worked out like that because it was broken down by the cooks at Bn HQ and the main meal was dumped into Dixies with water and heated up and this stew was distributed to the companies in 'hay boxes' (these were insulated carriers which kept the food hot for hours), so that we had a hot meal at least once a day every day. Sometimes we managed to get an untouched tin and in them we had bacon, steak and kidney pudding, Irish stew, beef and vegetables and also fruit cocktail, delicious rice pudding and even Xmas cake. They also had seven cigarettes a day per man, toilet paper, note paper and sweets. The ration lacked bulk, but was very high calorie and we could always make up for the bulk by soaking hard tack biscuits in the daily hot stew. If these rations failed to come up we had to fall back on to a can of bully and biscuits.

The weather improved and became dryer, but then we had another enemy, mosquitoes. They were big and so bad that we had to wear Balaclava helmets at night, and they would even bite through our heavy serge pants where they were stretched tight over the flesh beneath.

I should mention a little incident that demonstrates the futility of war. We had a sniper, 'Ticker' Owen, who made his way out to his hide in 'No man's land' and just as he got there a German soldier stepped out from behind a tree, both completely surprised at the other's presence, but Ticker reacted quickly, whipped out his cigarettes and offered one to his opposite number. The Jerry took one and both of them lit up, they sat down and had a smoke together and then each went his separate way.

Shortly after this incident we were relieved by the 8th Bn again and went for seven days rest on the banks of the Orne River. We were still within shellfire range and occasional bombing by the odd Jerry 'plane so we started digging in there and then we came across the body of a German soldier who had been buried. We thought he must have died at the hands of the Resistance, so we informed the Graves Registration people and they came along and took him away. A job I would not have liked doing. During the break we spent time lying up and sleeping, regaining strength and morale, and had visits to a cinema in Luc sur Mer and trips to the merchant ships lying offshore, where we got a real treat, white bread, cooked fresh on the ship that day. We managed to get out to the ships by scrounging rides on the DUKWs that were unloading stores from the ships and bringing them to dumps ashore. I also managed to visit the floating docks at Arromanches - what a piece of engineering and British ingenuity that was. All good things must come to an end so at the end of the seven days we were rotated back to the gloomy Bois de Bavent and back into our old slit trenches where we once again settled into our daily routine.

This routine was broken one morning when we saw a very large number of RAF bombers flying overhead. It was a thousand-bomber raid on Caen, and even though we were several miles from the raid the ground shook and it must have made the local Jerries nervous for they rained down mortar fire and Nebelwherfers (Moaning Minnies) on us. They hit our RAP, which was in a ditch at Bn HQ just a little ways back from me. I remember the Cpl medic had his stomach ripped open and he stitched it together with safety pins and shell dressings and then helped the other injured until he would allow himself to be evacuated. So Jack Chambers and I were very busy for a while using our one and only jeep to take wounded to the Field Dressing Station, just back a short way from the line.

Bob's farm was still the fly in the ointment and we were still unable to crack it and another attack took a few more of our men, but we kept up our night patrols, some of which were a little scary. By now our senses had become so acute that we could smell the German sausage and the body odour of the enemy, and we could skirt around them, if we wished, or, as we did on many an occasion, grab one and head back with him for interrogation. I still rode out with my nightly Sitreps and got chased by the mortars, I threw a cure into things at times and threw grenades behind me into the ditch while travelling at 60/70 mph; seemed to work for a while and then they smartened up and blanketed an area that I had to travel through. The REME people did a really good job of servicing my machine and getting me new tyres. Whenever I had a flat, they were just across the road from Bde HQ.

Then came the day when the breakout started. We had to advance towards Troarn and then Pont Le'Veque, where there was strong resistance for a while until the Bn managed to cross the river. At one point the CO told me to drive south down the side of the river and see if I could find a bridge intact and if I was able to cross and there seemed to be no enemy about to ride up north until I met up again with the Bn. So off I went as fast as my 1100cc BMW would travel, expecting the worst, but the man said have a go so have a go I did and I was able to report back as instructed that the area was clear.

After Pont Le'Veque we met some of the Free French fighters who promised to do a little scouting for us, but things changed in a hurry,

The Tale of Two Bridges

we had to dump our big packs and make a forced march to Pont Audemaur. We were given to understand that the Germans would try and make a kind of sideways break out of the Falaise Gap and if they did we were to defend and hold Pont Audemaur. We got into position and made ready for whatever might come along. I personally was in the Bishop's quarters, on the third floor with a very good view of the town from that height. Once settled in and advised where the other fellows were we waited, but fortunately nothing happened and about dusk some transport arrived and took us to a farm a few miles from Deauville. Luckily also nearby was a bath and delousing station. One went in at one end, dropped all one's clothing, was sprayed with DDT, then into a nice hot shower, then we were issued clothing and came out the other end with clean uniforms and underwear. Felt great too!

The next day we were allowed to go into Deauville, for some to buy a good meal or a couple of souvenirs, and for others a drink at the local estaminet. A couple of days later we embussed on transport and were taken all the way to Arromanches and shipped back to England, and to Bulford Barracks from whence we had departed several months before. After being kitted out with whatever gear we needed we received leave passes and I was off home to Yorkshire, where I surprised my family who thought I was still in France. What I should mention here is that when we finished leave and got back to barracks we then really noticed all the guys that were missing, some in hospital and of course others we left behind in France. One man in particular, Pat Pearson, who was my friend, was in Basingstoke Military Hospital (BMH), so I borrowed an open 15cwt truck and went to see him. His leg was pretty well banged up and still in plaster so we got him onto the truck and lashed his bad leg to the fender-mounted headlight and off we went to Salisbury to celebrate. Got him back later to the BMH in good shape, not that the Matron really agreed but she did comment, "Boys will be boys."!"

Gordon Brennan emigrated to Canada after the war
and lives there to this day

Personal account by Lieut D.C. [Tommy] FARR
Platoon Commander 'B' Company, 7 Para Bn

Lt Farr

"I will not deal with any action on the DZ as anything that happened there was an individual effort and, in some cases, was rather difficult to get an accurate picture.

The role of the company was:-
1. *To clear the village of LE PORT.*
2. *To clear and hold the wooded spur about 500 yards SW of LE PORT.*
3. *To establish a strong point on the WEST end of the canal bridge itself.*

We were briefed to carry out these tasks as follows:-

4 Platoon, under my command, task 1; 5 Platoon under Ted POOLE, task 2 and 6 Platoon, under Tommy THOMAS, task 3. This was slightly changed in the RV and 5 Platoon was detailed for the clearing of LE PORT and I, with 4 Platoon, was switched to the spur to the SW; this was necessary as I had not enough chaps to tackle the village. As we had all been briefed for all these three tasks this make no real difference and I was confident that my chaps would do their new task just as well as the one which they had expected to do.

The march to the objectives was, as far as we were concerned, uneventful. We crossed the bridges and marched up to the T junction, turned NORTH towards LE PORT and moved to where the wood joins the road on the LEFT hand side. I pushed a couple of scouts up the road to the first house in LE PORT and they reported back all quiet.

I then turned off the road through the wood and cleared it to the far end. No enemy encountered. I established a position at the WEST end of the wooded spur and had a fairly good field of fire to the WEST and NW. To the SOUTH it was not so good but, at least I could see down the gully which ran down the SOUTH edge of the wood.

At this stage I had about 12-14 chaps, who had managed to make the RV. Luckily I had three LMGs - thanks to the idea of dropping 4

The Tale of Two Bridges

per platoon - I organised into two sections and a strong platoon HQ, which was, to all intents and purposes, another section. Sgt BALDING had one section and Sgt CHERRY the other; I had the third myself, with Cpl CHAPMEN as gun corporal.

It was still dark when we took up positions on the end of the spur and as it was impossible to see all the ground we dug in fairly close together and I was able to control quite easily by verbal orders.

While digging in we had a few uncomfortable minutes. At first I thought we were being mortared, but as the bombs were bursting slap amongst us I could not understand how the Germans could see us if they were using a mortar. It was still dark and unless this was a target on which they already ranged I knew that they could not hit it. At last we worked it out, they were stick grenades.

There is a small ditch running across the field from LE PORT and this came right up to my platoon position. A German sergeant and one man had crawled along this with a lot of stick grenades and a machine gun. We found them about 10 yards away long this ditch from where they were throwing their stick grenades in amongst us. We returned with a 36 grenade and then Pte BRENNAN leapt up and finished them off with a burst of Sten.

Shortly after this we were under fire from a house in LE PORT. The Germans had a machine gun in an upstairs window and, having seen or heard our previous activity, they gave us an occasional burst. I could do little about this as 5 Platoon were somewhere in the village and I did not want to fire in that direction. 5 Platoon cleared up this trouble in time as they came through the village. I lost two men during these incidents. Pte PEPPER was wounded in the head by one of the stick grenades and had to be passed back and Pte ALLEN was wounded in the hand by the machine gun from LE PORT but carried on and stayed with us until I moved back.

Company HQ was back near the road (EAST of my position) and I was in touch with them by runner.

At first light we noticed a lot of movement in the open ground to the WEST of our position. We were attacked soon after this. The attack started by machine gun fire from the end of the hedgerow on our RIGHT front; we returned this and nothing much seemed to be happening. We then noticed a couple of sections of Germans

The Tale of Two Bridges

approaching from the WEST along the gully at the bottom of our spur (SOUTH side of it). They had not seen us and we were able to let them come right up to us before we opened fire. Unfortunately the cover was good and, although we got quite a few, some of them went to ground. The attack now developed from the direction of the original machine gun position and the Germans were advancing in ground which was dead to me. I reported the position and was ordered to withdraw to the road, which I duly did.

I lost a couple of chaps in getting out and one of them was a Bren gunner but, thanks to Sgt CHERRY, his weapon was not left. The enemy was now in the wood between us and company HQ but by keeping on the LE PORT side of the wood we were able to get back to the road where we consolidated with company HQ. The attack did not develop and, although a few shots were exchanged, the enemy did not attack company HQ from this direction.

Trouble at this time was coming from the BÉNOUVILLE direction (SOUTH) and there was a lot of activity at the T junction on the SOUTH side of company HQ.

The platoon was then moved back towards the bridge and occupied two houses just WEST of the canal bridge. Here our task was to cover the open ground to the SOUTH towards the CHATEAU DE BÉNOUVILLE. 'A' Company were having a lot of trouble in this area and we were moved back to cover any break-through by the enemy and to assist 6 Platoon in holding the bridge itself.

We remained in this position until the battalion was finally relieved late in the evening."

Note: The village of LE PORT referred to in Lt FARR's account is actually the NORTHERN end of the village of BÉNOUVILLE.

The Tale of Two Bridges

Personal account by Lieut W. [Walter] PARRISH, Platoon Commander 'C' Company 7 Para Bn

"When Butch [Lt. Lewendon] was prevented from taking his platoon of 'C' Company to NORMANDY I took over with two days in which to get to know the men and platoon task.

My plane, in which I was No 1, was unable to find the DZ until approximately 1 hour after the remainder of the battalion (say 0230hrs). When I arrived at the RV I found that what there was of the battalion had departed for an early crack at the Boche.

I gathered what there was of stragglers and went off to carry out my first task - to attack and clear houses at DZ side of the R ORNE (EAST) and then to clear area on the opposite side of the road, which was believed to contain enemy posts. When we arrived at 0315hrs these tasks had already been done.

I then crossed the bridge over the R ORNE en route for my second task, which seemed impossible to accomplish with my few men (about 10 including one sergeant, some of whom were from other platoons and even companies and were thus ignorant of the task). Nearing the canal bridge I was hailed by Bob KEEN [Keene] and given by him a few more of my own men and two light machine guns; I then had 2 light machine guns, 1 2-inch mortar and personal weapons among 14 other ranks including Sgt WILKES, one L/Cpl and one sniper, with full equipment. The plan called for communication by wireless but we had no wireless.

The news of the enemy in the area of BÉNOUVILLE was sparse and I was given Eric WOODMAN's task which meant proceeding down the WEST bank of the canal, as an outpost, in what appeared from aerial photographs to be a battery position. It was not known though whether this was occupied or not.

I started off in what must have been bright moonlight; I remember feeling almost naked and whatever the weather facts are I insist that it was moonlight. We were in two files proceeding quite slowly and stopping now and again to investigate noises which were never caused by German agency. Gathering boldness, by the time we reached the oil storage place (0430hrs) I should have been quite surprised to have been resisted although quite ready for it. The installation was in use but there was no sign of the users. Sending a recce party up a track which ran along its SOUTH side, in the meantime I had a large hole cut in the thickly meshed wire which surrounded the installation. A quick look round inside revealed only absentees. The reconnaissance party returned and reported that the track joined a road, that there were no Germans about and the wire did indeed surround the storage tanks (0500hrs).

Time was running short. The ground was tricky with wire fences and ditches and it was with a sense of urgency that I began the last leg of our approach to the outpost position.

Mistaking in my haste the position of the gun site we began to penetrate a tangle of bramble bushes which lay on the LEFT of our line of approach. This was, to date, the greatest enemy we had met. By the time we were extricated the war was a distant thing, the drop was forgotten, the enemy a vague thing and officers, especially me, were an anathema.

Luckily the objective was next door and we occupied it - it was deserted - just as dawn was rosily flushing the EAST, or was it the WEST? WILKES took a section to face the road which was bout 350 yards distant and the L/Cpl (whose name I forget) faced the sandpit bounding the NORTH of my position and overlooking a bend in the canal. I further placed two men close to the canal bank, while I had a small HQ in a pit in the approximate centre. An LMG was placed to cover our rear as I expected to be cut off from the battalion.

These dispositions were hardly made when D day was heralded by long and large explosions from seawards (I could just see the tower of the church at OUISTREHAM from my command post). Clouds of dust and smoke, tinged gently to roseate hues by the fading dawn, towered high above the church, showing how close we had approached to the coast.

Throughout the next hour there was little to occupy our attention but battle noises from the NORTH. Large bangs gave place to smaller and more frequent ones. These in turn became rattles of small arms and the louder ones were identifiable as field guns and other pieces suitable for land warfare. This was really all conjecture but it was very heartening as it told of a foothold gained and of progress being made.

The first incident to concern us was the arrival, all unknowing, of three civilians with one bicycle. They approached to within 100 yards before they saw us and then began to depart. A shot over their heads brought them back and the usual emotional scene followed. I was kissed on one cheek, but managed to save the other one. These Frenchmen had no news, so I parked them in the small quarry which was behind my command post and forgot them until very late that day.

Then something important happened. Driven inland from the bombardment, three vessels, of the fishing type, came up the canal. The decks were armed with what was either an AA LMG, or a light shell firing piece, manned by men in the uniform of, I believe, the GAF.

As the vessels came level with my canal bank post my men there raked the decks with Sten fire; four, or five, enemy were seen to drop and it is difficult to see how they could have escaped death from that range. It was about 30 yards. The ships went on up the canal towards the bridge and another hot reception. The invasion noises persisted and small arms fire could now be heard quite distinctly.

Just below my platoon position on the bank of the canal was a small landing stage. It could not well be covered from any part of the outpost and I had not enough men to cover it in any way. Another vessel came up the canal about 0815hrs and moored at this landing stage.

I had it watched, but apparently not sufficiently well to prevent some of the crew from landing. The first intimation I had that landings had been made was a report of the approach up the centre sandpit of a large bush. Slowly it was making its way towards the L/Cpl's position. I rushed my sniper to a position where he could shoot at it but unfortunately I was still afraid that I might kill innocent Frenchmen. I had the sniper put his bullet beside the bush and not into it. There began our misfortunes, which were to last throughout most of the day.

The LMG gunner, who was covering my rear, was sniped from the sandpit and killed. The gun was retrieved as a matter of course by a man, whose name I forget. Bullets began to whistle through the trees which were between my command post and the sandpit. I had insufficient men to do anything but lie low and snipe when opportunity offered.

A further section arrived from battalion HQ of about 7 men with another LMG. I am not at all sure the time when they arrived but it must have been about 0900hrs. I used them to thicken up the established positions and sent the LMG to WILKES.

My progress, when inspecting the positions, was made difficult by the flying bullets. To the nearer positions I either crawled or ran very hard. The L'Cpl's most effective post was at the sandpit end of a short tunnel. The mouth of this tunnel overlooked the sandpit and a man was constantly on the lookout from it.

I always made a point of looking out there too but it was only when a casualty occurred at that point that I decided to do something about the nuisance.

The casualty was a man called, I believe, Agar. On the occasion of one of my visits he looked out to see if the coast was clear when be sank back into my arms with a bullet in his head. I gave him all the aid I could and despatched a runner to ask for help for him and to report my situation to battalion HQ. My quiet outpost was now so uncomfortable that I just had to do something about it.

Giving instructions for redisposition and handing over to Sgt WILKES I carried out a LEFT flanking attack into the sandpit with about four men, under cover of 2-inch mortar smoke. The approach round the edge of the sandpit was easy and safe. When we reached the point at which we must descend into the pit though we found that the descent would be observable from the landing stage and also from a house which lay behind it (1130hrs). The route lay beside some brambles which gave no cover from the enemy and, indeed, effectively prevented us from taking cover if he should fire. Nothing interrupted our descent however and, splitting up into pairs, we searched the bottom of the sandpit.

The enemy was not there. We searched the scrub thoroughly and the hummocks of the pit, one covering the other forward, until we reached our positions. The redispositions were made with particular sniping strength covering a part of the landing stage, which anybody landing must cross. I remember that my partner in the search was McCARTHY. During the next two hours or so my snipers must have accounted for up to four enemy attempting to cross from, or to, the moored vessel.

The time when the vessels were fired on at the bridge will probably be known but I estimate that two of these three ships approached my positions, from upstream, at about 1430hrs. The decks were deserted; disappointingly so as I had arranged a very hot reception for them. Oh for a PIAT! The ships passed and they too moored at the landing stage. Warning the snipers to be on the alert I expected a recurrence of the trouble I had had from the first vessel to moor. Whether they had had

The Tale of Two Bridges

enough or whether they were planning something more devilish was a question that gave me much food for thought.

Close watching discovered nothing for more than two hours until a great noise of small arms and louder explosions of grenades pointed to a crossing having been made, or attempted, just below the landing stage. I could not see anything but the noise persisted so long in the same place that I concluded that it came from the ships themselves. A reconnaissance patrol was obviously the answer but this time it must be an NCO's patrol. The L'Cpl (I wish I could remember his name; I later met him as a sergeant) took two men to investigate and report as quickly as possible.

The answer was that the enemy had set fire to the vessels and the noise was that of the ammunition burning. No enemy could be found and no dead 'uns either. I had given the patrol instructions that the ships must not be boarded in case of booby traps. Perhaps the "stiffs" were to be found aboard.

The platoon score was distinctly gratifying now. Besides the enemy casualties inflicted we had captured three vessels which I must now describe as men of war. Surely no other parachute unit, or any other sort of unit for that matter, had accomplished that much?

I sent another runner off to report this and the fact that Agar (?) was still in the tunnel, looking far gone by this time, but as comfortable as he could be made. The previous runner had not returned, and, fearing that we were indeed cut off, I cautioned this one to use all the fieldcraft he had picked up in training. I didn't believe for one moment that he had learned any but he must then have wished that he had. He not only made the journey, but returned and brought with him two medical orderlies for the casualty (1830hrs).

Things were quiet now and I remembered the three civilians and the bicycle whom I had caused to be parked in the quarry. I sent them away and they appeared quite grateful for their day-long incarceration.

Battle noises were now well inland from my position and most of them appeared to come from the battalion positions at the bridge. On the high ground away across the river I could see ant-like lines of commandos who must have crossed the bridges. It was puzzling to see them and to hear the sounds of heavy firing coming from the bridges. From a high piece of ground near my command post I risked looking to see what was happening. Puffs of smoke from phosphorous grenades appeared every now and again and through each puff ran tiny figures of men crossing to the EAST side.

I was then visited by Capt TODD. He was in despondent mood and informed me that the battalion had long been pushed back from its original positions and had concentrated around the canal bridge. Every enemy attack had been repulsed but casualties were heavy and, indeed, my platoon was the most complete at that time. I was needed, if I remember correctly, as a sort of reserve force and, according to TODD, the odds were pretty fearful. We were away from the outpost within ten minutes (1930hrs) and proceeded towards the battalion in three files.

Our first sight of them was of men resting beneath a wall; lots of men and happy looking men at that. Were they happy because after a day of stiff fighting, they were giving place in the glory queue to me and my well rested men? Firing was desultory and more men were resting there when I reached battalion HQ and reported to Major STEELE-BAUME, the second-in-command. The atmosphere was almost one of peace.

I was ordered to rest my men and wait for orders. While we were there we were attacked by the Royal Engineers, but they were beaten off. I also learned of the 'A' Company saga. In fact, I heard so much about the battles of everybody else that I could not bring myself to tell of the part played by my little platoon.

Just before dusk Lt-Col PINE-COFFIN ordered me to take over 'A' Company, which was then sadly depleted and was without any of its own officers."

Note: Personalities referred to in Lt PARRISH's account:-
Butch - Lt LEWENDON from whom he took over the platoon a few hours before the drop. Bob Keen - Capt R.A. KEEN [mis-spelling of KEENE], acting commander of 'C' Company 7 Para Bn. Eric Woodman - Lt E. WOODMAN, platoon commander 'C' Company 7 Para Bn. Capt Todd - Assistant Adjutant 7 Para Bn.
Lt PARRISH is wrong in his timings in certain cases. The two gun boats that came up the canal as far as the bridge, where one was knocked out, did so at 1000hrs and NOT 1430hrs as he states.

The Tale of Two Bridges

Ron Perry – MMG Pl

"We departed from Fairford in a Stirling aircraft. I was No 20 in a stick of 21, composed of men from the MMG platoon and the mortar platoon. My recollection is that there were 40 men in each platoon divided amongst four aircraft on a 50-50 basis with two Vickers guns and two mortars in containers with each aircraft. In the event none were recovered and the two platoons lost over half their effectives on the drop and in subsequent actions. KILLED, WOUNDED or MISSING.

Bill French was No 21 and he and I went forward at take off into the cramped cabin of the navigator (in fact the master navigator) who was concerned throughout, with the Eureka Rebecca system for accurate navigation. I had earlier that year trained with this pathfinder system while with the 'I' Section.

Ron Perry

From take-off I was linked to the inter-comm, thus being privy to the aircrew's comments and instructions, which continued throughout the flight. There was a particular call from the rear gunner about enemy aircraft; as we approached the French coast there were reports from the crew of heavy flak, and the noise externally greatly increased as the aircraft was hit. 'Green light' on and we were shuffling forward to the exit hole towards the rear of the aircraft. Percy Fear and Ray Dye were momentarily silhouetted against the ground as they exited, highlighted against lines of criss-crossing red and green tracer, which appeared continuous. Then I was out!

Almost at once I felt pain in one hand and the small of my back, but what I was far more concerned about was the machine gun fire striking my chute. I seemed to be at low height, the aircraft was receding. I could not see other chutes or recognise landmarks. I fell into a deep ditch when my chute draped over telephone (or power) lines running alongside a track bordering the ditch which was high in nettles, brambles and tree roots. This cover helped me, for the parachute remained suspended over the lines. The periphery was flickering with flame and attracted gunfire. There was difficulty in getting out of the harness and I became aware of three or four figures approaching from across the field, framed against the skyline. More machine gun fire and these figures, whether friend or foe, dropped from sight.

Bill French appeared closely followed by Nick Archdale, both had landed in, or alongside, the ditch. We set off, meeting Freddie Fricker, Norman Reynolds and two or three others, all from the same aircraft, northwards, along the track, collecting a member of 8 Para who had landed in a tree. In a few hundred yards the track terminated at the foot of the river bridge where the road ran westwards to the canal bridge. The battalion's call sign was evident - a bugle call - an indication of the direction to take.

Great activity approaching and at the canal bridge. An armoured car destroyed, its fuel escaping and running across the roadway on fire. Constant machine gun and small arms fire, the rounds ricocheting from the frame work. Norman Reynolds and I crossed the bridge and joined men of the Ox and Bucks LI in a German gun position on the Bénouville side. We remained here until dawn when Nick Archdale collected a group of us - perhaps eight or ten in number - and we advanced along the elevated towpath northwards towards the coast. I believe the intention was to reinforce 'B' or 'C' Company further down the riverside. In 200 yards or so we attracted enemy attention and returned fire. We left the exposed towpath, going into marshy ground up to our knees. We entered a line of small cottages running parallel to the towpath and the river at about 150 yards distant and on the other side there was an access track from orchards leading down to a roadway, between buildings. (Later I realised the road led from Bénouville, crossed past the Le Port church and small paved area or place, and joined with another road leading from the direction of Ouistreham.)

Nick and I turned the corner of the buildings on the left-hand side, with Freddie Fricker on the right-hand side. We were immediately fired upon, the rounds ricocheting from the stonework between Nick and I, which forced us to retire back around the corner. The fire was heavy and constant. (Later in the morning we found Hayward, the RSM's Batman, shot dead beside a Bren gun in the opposite hedge. I recovered the Bren.) There was a door in the flank of the corner building which I entered. I

The Tale of Two Bridges

climbed a stairway inside leading to a door at its head, entering a bedroom with a couple asleep on a bed who sat up and became aware of my presence and the increasing crescendo of noise outside. Both the man and woman were unclothed and, it seemed, completely unaware of the events occurring. Immediate confusion until my rudimentary command of the French language brought enlightenment. The man then disappeared down the staircase, reappearing with a bottle, which we proceeded to empty whilst toasting the allies. I rejoined the war some time later to find the lads 'digging in' within the orchard. Their various enquiries as to where I had been went unanswered.

We remained in these positions until evening, by which time we had witnessed the arrival of the main glider force - also leading elements of men of the Royal Warwicks. We moved at dusk back across the bridge. I bivouacked in a field alongside the road leading to the river bridge. Next day we dug positions along the road from Ranville crossroads, which leads to Sallenelles, using a high bank with excellent view of the dropping zone and the wooded high ground beyond. We were in company with the Commandos, also digging in. There were numerous incidents during the next two to three days and nights - notably German aircraft coming in low across our front, 'strafing' and attempting to bomb the bridge.

We were issued with two Vickers machine guns and I believe four No 3" mortars, from an ordnance area set up in a quarry, together with .303 ammo, 3" mortar bombs and a trolley to haul them. We used these weapons to great effect throughout that morning when a heavy German counter attack was launched from the high ground across the dropping zone, using the debris of crashed gliders and other wreckage as cover. The mortars were in constant action with the MMGs firing on open sights and at times a swinging traverse. Bill Watkiss and I manned one of the Vickers, having set up in a previously dug slit trench. (I have not seen Bill since leaving the army, but each Christmas I receive his card and he always reminds me of our joint experience.) At one point we were joined by a Brigadier, from the Tank Brigade, whose Sherman tanks had crossed the bridge and were arriving in the battle area. Whilst awaiting their arrival the Brigadier took a turn to fire the Vickers. Tragically five of the tanks were hit and destroyed as soon as they appeared, probably by 88mm SP guns, which plagued us throughout the morning.

By midday, or soon after, the Bn advanced from Ranville area DZ along the road leading to Herouvillette and Escoville, successfully clearing the orchards and close ground on the flank of the road, causing considerable casualties to the Germans. This clearance was later described as a textbook operation. By the early evening we had dug in amongst the heavily wooded ground approaching Breville, attracting German fire during the night. There had been rainfall since the late afternoon and onwards. I was one of those directed to return to the scene of the afternoon's operation to collect identification from the many German dead.

On Sunday the main assault on Breville was launched by a mixed force of 12 Para Bn, 1st Canadian Para, Devons from the Airlanding Brigade. These units, particularly 12 Para, sustained heavy losses. The 5th Bn Black Watch took part in this battle moving ahead from positions held by 7 Para. We were in Herouvillette for a few days before taking over positions in the heavily wooded Bois de Bevant from 8 Para Bn. We remained in these positions for seven or eight days. There was considerable activity, including the first attack on Bob's farm - named after Bob Keene, who at the time was commanding 'B' Coy. One of our MMG positions was destroyed by mortar fire, four men being killed and two or three others being seriously wounded.

Together with Jack 'Tubby' Harris, Henry 'Flash' Baker, Percy Hatton, Hart and 'Taffy' Harris, we manned a position at the junction of two hedgerows, where a track and a gully led through orchards and thick trees to Bob's farm. Nick Archdale established an FO point in the orchard behind our position where we set up a Vickers gun and an MG 42 in close proximity. Mortar fire, including shelling from the rocket multi-launchers, was a regular feature. On one particular night Tubby Harris, Hatton and Hart were all wounded. After seven or eight days we returned to a rest area close to the Orne Canal. It was now three weeks since the D-Day landings. 'Jock' Pearson's 8 Bn took over from us and after three or four days we returned to relieve them once again, this time to make a second attempt to take Bob's farm; again unsuccessfully.

Although my recollections of our times in the Bois de Bevant are somewhat hazy, I believe we spent three separate periods there - always lively and often most uncomfortable, not least because of the myriad mosquitoes that plagued us at dusk and during the night and the stench

The Tale of Two Bridges

of dead animals. At our first visit we had buried our dead machine gunners in some haste behind our positions, due to being under mortar fire. On a return visit we were required to disinter them three weeks later for removal to Ranville. Sometime in late July we moved into forward positions originally held by Commandos in the Sallenelles area.

In August the division moved forward on the breakout to the Seine. The axis of advance for 5 Parachute Brigade was along the main road from Caen, via Troarn, Dozule and Putot En Auge, Pont Audemer to Le Havre. We had sharp actions, notably at Putot En Auge and Pont Le Eveque, the Bn sustaining casualties. We had received reinforcements during July and August, namely men returning from being wounded in the early days - some Para men being posted from the UK and notably men from the King's Shropshire Light Infantry. We reached Pont Audemer, where we again sustained casualties - shellfire and mortar fire causing casualties in the mortar platoon, Sgt Fred Fricker amongst others.

Withdrawn from action we went into bivouac near the coast, close to Deauville and Trouville. Two or three days later we were trucked to Arromanches and the following morning by LCI to a troopship. The journey to Southampton was wild and stormy and took several hours, mainly throughout the night. Train to Bulford sidings and return to Gordon Barracks with many bunks now vacant."

Footnote: Ron was 20 years old when he jumped at Normandy. He had volunteered from the Rifle Brigade. He joined 7 (LI) Parachute Battalion after it was formed from the 10th Somerset (LI) and was posted to 8 platoon 'C' Company. His Platoon Commander was Lt Grayburn. They were on the same draft at Hardwick Hall and marched the 58 miles to Ringway to complete their parachute training. Lt Grayburn was one of the men who the 7th Battalion 'lost' when he was transferred to the 2nd Bn 1st Airborne Division. He was later killed in action on the bridge at Arnhem and was awarded the VC for his gallantry.

Ron then went on to serve in the Intelligence Section before he was transferred to the machine gun platoon just before Operation Overlord. He reflects, *"Although I am not superstitious with a CO called Pine-Coffin, Percy Fear - No.18 Pokey Dye - No 19, myself jumping at No 20, this has given me food for thought."*

Personal account by Major J.N. [Nigel] Taylor, MC, OC 'A' Company, 7 Para Bn

"We moved off from the DZ at about, I should imagine, 0230hrs and contacted the brigade commander on the bridges. After a few words with him we went over the bridges, seeing HOWARD on the way.

At this time I had very few men, only about 30. I got another 20 on the other side of the bridges; we then cut across the back of the Maire. After searching that we went up the CAEN road into BÉNOUVILLE.

Major Nigel Taylor, MC
2nd-in-Command

I had Sgt VILLIS' platoon leading, then company HQ with BOWYER with me and his platoon behind, then David HUNTER and his platoon. As VILLIS' leading man got to the main cross roads of the village a motor cyclist came round the corner from the EAST and down the road towards us. Everybody fired at him and he crashed just behind me. Bill BOWYER's runner, or batman, fired at him too when he was on the ground and unfortunately Bill was hit and died later.

I ordered VILLIS into the houses on the SOUTH end of the village and HUNTER into the farm buildings to the WEST. Company HQ went into the gardens of the houses on the other side of the road and the remains of BOWYER's platoon into the houses to the EAST of that.

Things were fairly quiet until first light. We could then hear vehicles moving (tracked) on the CAEN road and were ready for armour. The enemy started up just before first light (about 0400hrs?) firing down the road with his SP guns and trying to infiltrate infantry round our WEST (RIGHT) flank. The latter were effectively held off all day by HUNTER.

The houses on the forward edge (SOUTH) of the village became untenable because we had nothing with the range to keep the SPs quiet, so VILLIS had to be retired into houses further back. The Boche then penetrated into the village with SPs, tanks and an armoured car.

Company HQ had, by this time, moved to the RIGHT of the road (WEST) and so had the remains of VILLIS' platoon, I had to move these later as I could hear the battle going on in 'B' Company's area and, on one occasion, a German Mk IV tank came through from that direction. This was slightly shaking, but we got it with about 4 gammons and were pleased to see him on fire. The SP was still firing straight down the road but couldn't hit any of us, except Jim and I!

The position then was that we were holding a sort of reverse slope position behind the village. It was remarkably effective. The Germans couldn't get at us but if he tried to infiltrate we had the field of fire and got him immediately. Our men realised their position in a remarkable way and were extremely alive to the danger of letting any enemy get into a fire position. We had snipers in odd houses who gave the general run of the battle by shouting so that most could hear (we were in an extremely tight locality). Mortar fire was not particularly effective against us but, of course, casualties grew slowly and rather inexorably during the day.

In the afternoon we were greatly cheered to see two SHERMANS come up to us - the place was alive with yellow smoke, yellow triangles and red berets on sticks - but without contacting us they went straight on and were never seen by us again. Things were quiet for about half an hour after their appearance. I believe they got brewed up further down the road.

The Germans never knew what strength we had. They never really launched an all out attack as we would understand it. Plenty of fires, yes, and Verey lights but no men or bayonets. We expected it every time things brewed up, but it never came. If they had really tried to outflank us they would have made it extremely awkward for us.

We were eventually relieved in the evening and our wounded got out by the scout cars. The Germans never fired at these wounded being evacuated."

Major TAYLOR was badly wounded in the leg early in the action but continued to influence the battle from a stretcher.

Active command was exercised by Capt J.J. WEBBER, the company second-in-charge, who although wounded himself more than once retained the use of his legs. He is the officer referred to as Jim in TAYLOR's account.

The officer referred to as HOWARD was Major HOWARD the commander of the "coup de main" party.

Gammons are the special tank busting bomb carried by parachutists. Named after Lieut GAMMON, himself a parachutist, who invented it. It utilised the two pounds of plastic explosive which is carried in action by all parachutists. It was an effective weapon provided the thrower was within close range of the tank.

An un-named German Private, on guard in Normandy on the night of 6th June, 1944, remembers the following:

There was a strong wind, thick cloud cover, and the enemy aircraft had not bothered us more that day than usual. But then - in the night - the air was full of innumerable planes. We thought, "What are they demolishing tonight?" But then it started. I was at the wireless set myself. One message followed the other. "Parachutists landed here - gliders reported there", and finally "Landing craft approaching." Some of our guns fired as best they could. In the morning a huge naval force was sighted - that was the last report our advanced observation posts could send us, before they were overwhelmed. And it was the last report we received about the situation. It was no longer possible to get an idea of what was happening. Wireless communications were jammed, the cables cut and our officers had lost grasp of the situation. Infantrymen who were streaming back told us that their position on the coast had been overrun or that the few 'bunkers' in our sector had either been shot up or blown to pieces.

Words of songs which were normally sung or whistled by the troops as they marched, or as in the song that follows, jumped [this was generally sung to the tune of 'The Mountains of Mourne']:

> Oh Mary, this Tattons a wonderful sight,
> With the paratroops jumping by day and by night.
> They land on potatoes, and barley, and corn,
> And there's gangs of them wishing they'd never been born,
> At least, when I asked them that's what I was told,
> The jumping is easy, slow pairs leaves them cold,
> They said that they'd rather bale out of the moon,
> Than jump anymore from that awful balloon.

Another song which was sung at top voice, to the tune of 'John Brown's Body', was also popular and would have been sung as they marched:

> 'Is everybody happy' said the Sergeant looking up
> Our hero answered 'Yes' and then they hooked him up
> He jumped into the slipstream and he twisted twenty times,
>   He ain't going to jump no more
> Chorus: Glory, Glory, what a hell of a way to die
>   (Repeat three times)
> And he ain't going to jump no more.
>
> He counted loud, he counted long, and waited for the shock
> He felt the wind, he felt the sir, he felt the awful drop
> He pulled the lines, the silk came down,
>   and wrapped around his legs
> And he ain't going to jump no more.
>   Chorus
>
> The days he lived, and loved, and laughed,
>   kept running through his mind
> He thought about the medicos, and wondered what they'd find
> He thought about the girl back home, the one he'd left behind,
> And he ain't going to jump no more.
>   Chorus

The Tale of Two Bridges

The lines all wrapped around his neck,
the 'D' rings broke his Dome
The lift webs wrapped themselves in knots
around each skinny bone
The canopy became his shroud, as he hurtled to the ground
And he ain't going to jump no more.
Chorus

The ambulance was on the spot, the jeeps were running wild
The medicos they clapped their hands,
and rolled their sleeves and smiled
For it had been a week or so since that a chute had failed
And he ain't going to jump no more.
Chorus

He hit the ground, the sound was 'splat',
the blood went spurting high
His pals were heard to say, 'Oh what a pretty way to die'
They rolled him up still in his chute,
and poured him from his boots.
And he ain't going to jump no more.
Chorus

There was blood upon the lift webs,
there was blood upon his chute
Blood that came a'trickling from the paratrooper's boots
And there he lay like jelly, in the welter of his gore
And he ain't going to jump no more. R.I.P.

A slightly less gory song, sung to the tune of 'Knees Up Mother Brown':

Jumping through the hole,
Jumping through the hole,
I'll always keep my trousers clean
When jumping through the hole.

The knowledge of these songs is attributable to Sid Mundy.

The Tale of Two Bridges

DÉPARTEMENT DU CALVADOS

MAIRIE
de
BÉNOUVILLE
(14790)

Tél. 31 44 62 01
Fax 31 95 30 26

Document kindly supplied
by Tony Lycett

Le Conseil Municipal en sa séance du 29 juillet 1996, a pris la délibération suivante :

" En reconnaissance du courage de ses officiers et de ses soldats et à la mémoire de ceux qui ont donné leur vie pour la libération de Bénouville dès les premières heures du 6 juin 1944,"

Le Conseil Municipal décide d'inscrire le 7ème bataillon du régiment de parachutistes sur le livre d'or de la commune en tant que citoyen d'honneur.

During the session held on 29 july 1996, the Town Council has adopted the following decision :

"In gratitude for the courage of its officers and its soldiers, and in memory of those who gave their life for the liberation of Bénouville from the very first hours of D.Day,"

the Town Council has decided to register the 7th battalion of paratroopers regiment in the golden book of the town as freeman of the town.

Le maire,
A. NIVAULT

Lest we forget

Colonel R.G. Pine-Coffin, DSO, MC
talking to pilgrims in Normandy in 1955

Some acronyms used in this book

18 set	Radio/Wireless
38 set	Radio/Wireless
68 set	Radio/Wireless
2 I/C	Second in Command
A/L	Air Landing
ACC	Army Catering Corps
ADJT	Adjutant
ADMN	Administration
ADMS	Assistant Director Medical Services
ADOS	Assistant Director Ordnance Services
AMB	Ambulance
AMMO	Ammunition
APTC	Army Physical Training Corps
ARMD	Armoured
ATT	Attached
BDE	Brigade
BN	Battalion
BRIG	Brigadier
BTY	Battery
C/SGT	Colour Sergeant
CAPT	Captain
CDO	Commando
CND	Canadian
CO	Commanding Officer
COL	Colonel
COMD	Commander
COY	Company
CPL	Corporal
CQMS	Company Quarter Master Sergeant
CRA	Commander Royal Artillery
CRASC	Commander Royal Army Service Corps
CRE	Commander Royal Engineers
CSM	Company Sergeant Major
DET	Detachment
DIV	Division
DOUBLE	Run
DRA	Divisional rest area
DUKW	Amphibious Truck
DVR	Driver
DZ	Dropping Zone
FD	Field
FOO	Forward Observation Officer
GNR	Gunner
GOC	General Officer Commanding
GP	Group

HE	High Explosive
HQ	Headquarters
IO	Intelligence Officer
INDEP	Independent
INF	Infantry
INT	Intelligence
L/A	Light Artillery
L/CPL	Lance Corporal
LCI	Landing Craft Infantry
LI	Light Infantry
LMG	Light Machine Gun
LT	Lieutenant
MMG	Medium Machine Gun
MO	Medical Officer
OP	Observation Post
ORD	Orderly
OTC	Officers Training Corps
PARA	Parachute
PIAT	Projectile Infantry Anti Tank
PKS	Park (s)
PL	Platoon
PRO	Provost (Police)
PTE	Private
QM	Quartermaster
RA	Royal Artillery
RAMC	Royal Army Medical Corps
RAOC	Royal Army Ordnance Corps
RAP	Regimental Aid Post
RASC	Royal Army Service Corps
RE	Royal Engineers
RECCE	Recconnaisance
REGT	Regiment
REME	Royal Electrical & Mechanical Engineers
RQMS	Regimental Quartermaster Sergeant
RSM	Regimental Sergeant Major
RTU	Returned to Unit
SCF	Senior Chaplain to the Forces
SEC	Section
SGT	Sergeant
SIGS	Signals
SO	Signals Officer
SPR	Sapper
SQN	Squadron
TRG	Training
VC	Victoria Cross - Highest award for bravery
WKSHPS	Workshops

The Tale of Two Bridges

Index

(p) = photograph

Agar, Pte	159,160	Carew, Tim	23
Allen, Pte	154	Chamberlain, Neville	xiii
Amey, Sgt	xv,45	Chambers, Pte J.	29,51,146,148,151
Amery, Leo	xiii	Chapmen, Cpl J.	154
Archdale, Lt Nick	ix,xiv,41(p),50,52, 53,60,65,101,105, 116, 118,163,165	Cherry, Sgt	154,155
		Churchill, Winston	xiii(p),1
Atkinson, Lt R.N.	xv,46,47,84,180	Copp, RSM Johnny	126
		Cornell, Pte/Sgt E. DCM	xv,65(p),78,90
Baker, Henry 'Flash'	165	Coulthard, L/Cpl A.J.	91,180
Balding, Sgt L.G.	154,180		
Barker, Maj Gen	113,114		
Barlow, Col Hilary N.	10,117,127,128, 129	Davey, L/Cpl R.J.	40
		Davis, Pte	80
Bartle, Cpl	79	Dennys, Lt Col K.G.G.	5
Bartlett, Maj	xv,30,68,89	Durbin, CSM F.E.	xv,79,180
Bettle, Cpl/Sgt J.D.	xv,80	Dye, Ray	162,166
Bowler, Lt J.A.	xiv,60,180		
Bowyer, Lt/Capt W.	xiv,55,167,180		
Bradley, Gen Omar	9(p)	Edwards, Dennis	34
Braithwaite, Capt B.R.	xv,66,99	Elvin, Pte W. 'Bill'	19(p),21,22,27,45, 48,55
Bramall, Field Marshal	117		
Brennan, Pte G.	144(p),152,154	Emery, L/Cpl L.M.	69
Browning, Lt Gen F.A.M.	11	Essex-Lopreski, Lt P. (Surgeon)	4
Buller, Gen R.	126	Evans, Pte S.	91
Bush, CQMS H.J.	xv,81		
Bushell, Pte/Cpl H.R.	55,180	Farr, Lt D.C.	xv,44(p),79,127, 153(p)
Butler, Pte Arnold	90		
Butler, Pte John	34,149	Fay, Sgt V.C.	44,99,180
Butterwood, Pte R.	87		

176

Fear, Pte/Sgt Percy	xv,162,166	Hatton, Pte P.	165
Flavell, Brig E.	1	Hayward, L/Cpl S.D.	163,181
Fleming, Lt R.	10	Hill, Brig S.J.L.	xvi,6
Follett, L/Cpl R.	121(p)	Hill, Lt M.R.	xiv,55,60,180
Formby, George & Beryl	94,95(p)	HM King and Queen	xiii,130(p)
Forster, Lt A.N.D.	77	Howard, Lt	83,95
Fortnum, Capt/QMS R.P.H.	xiv,93(p)	Howard, Maj J.	15,17,32,33,34(p), 35,39,53,131,132, 145,146,167,169
Fraser, Maj F.	16(p)		
French, Sgt W.	xiv,118(p),120,162, 163	Humble, Pte F.	xiv,80,81
Fricker, Sgt Fred	xiv,116,134(p),137, 163,166	Hunter, Lt D.	xiv,167
		Hutchinson, Cpl T.	44
Gale, Maj Gen R.N.	xvi,1,8(p),9,11,14, 53,54,74,88,91, 103,106,110,113, 114,130,132	Jamieson, Pte George	138,139,140
		Johnson, RSM G.W.	xiv,81(p)
Garnervin, Andre	1	Keene, Capt/Maj R.A. 'Bob'	xv,30,31(p),66, 77(p),90,91,156, 161,165
Gammon, Lt R.J.	40		
Gould, Tom	31	Keyes, Sir Roger	xiii
Grayburn, Lt H. VC	166	Killeen, Cpl Tommy	40(p),42,50,145
Green, Pte K.	80		
Gurney, Sgt E. 'Eddy'	22,26,32,35,38,39	Ladd, Alan	23(p)
		Lake, C/Sgt Sammy	xv,117
Halifax, Lord	xiii	Lateur, Lt R. de	86
Hardwick, Pte	82	Le Cheminant, signaller	90
Harper, Sgt C.	xv,80	Lenormand, L.S.	1
Harris, Jack 'Tubby'	165	Lewendon, Lt P.	19(p),20,156,161
Harris, 'Taffy'	165	Lewis, Pte	95,96
Hart, Pte E.J.	165		

Liddell, Pte D.S.	81		Parry, Capt G.	xiv,20,36,55,181
Loch, Lt J.H.	10		Patterson, Lt W.F. (Canadian)	83(p),91
Lovat, Brig The Lord	xvi,15,50,51,121, 146		Pearson, Lt Col T.	xvi,140,117,165
			Pearson, Pte P.	149,152
Lucas, Sgt T.J.	xv,90,91		Pepper, Pte R.E.	154
Lycett, Pte T.	ix,172		Perry, C/Sgt Ron	ix,118,162(p),166
			Poett, Brig J.H.N.	xvi,9(p),19,35, 56(p),67,90,95, 112,129
McCara, Pte J.	38			
McCarthy, Sgt C.	159		Poole, Lt E.	xv,44,77,78,79,80, 123(p),128,133
McDonald, Lt I.	32,42,53,71			
McGee, Pte M.J. DCM	39(p),40,181		Porter, Pte J.	141
Mills, Lt H.R.	xiv,16,36,56,57(p), 75,86,98,101		Porter, S.C.	141,142
			Prentice, Sgt/CSM J.	xv,81,90
Mold, Dr E.	138		Price, Rear Gunner A.E.	181
Montgomery, Field Marshall	xii(p),130		Price, L/Cpl S.	91,182
Moran, Pte J.	28		Purdy, Pte W.	80
Mundy, Lt S.	3,171			
			Reason, Pte P.	149
Neale, Maj R.	xv,44,65,66,127		Reid, Maj 'Tiger'	31(p)
Nicholls, Lt K.J.H.	110		Reynolds, L/Cpl E.N.	163
Norman, Sgt D.	89		Ricketts, Sgt W.	89,90
			Rogers, Lt F.J.H.	xiv,28,29
O'Sullivan, Pte J.	60,108		Rogers, Capt J.	110(p)
Owen, 'Ticker'	150		Rommel, Field Marshall	69(p)
			Rugge Price, Major	63
Pape, Lt J.C. (Canadian)	83,89,90,104,105			
Parr, Cpl Willy	34		Shinner, Pte J.S.	141
Parrish, Lt/Capt W.F.	xv,20,34,63(p),68, 71,80,81,156,161		Skolly, Pte G.	72

Smith, Sgt R.J.	82		Wagstaffe, Capt J.A.	xiv,36(p),138
Squirrel, Lt Col J.G.	1		Wallis, Maj D.W.	129
Starke, Pte R.A.	28		Watkiss, Cpl W.	164
Steele-Baume, Maj E.	30(p),35,66,117,130		Webber, Capt J.J.	xiv,52,53,168
			Went, Capt/Maj J.D.	xiv,83(p)
Stenner, Sgt	10,182		Westby, Pte J.	149
Strudwick, Pte E.S.	69		Weston, Pte R.C.	79
Styles, Pte G.	28		Whittingham, L/Cpl P.	38,182
Sykes, Sgt Eric 'Bill'	2,24,28		Wilkes, CSM W.	xv,156,157,158,159
			Wilson, Cpl W.C.	87,105,182
Tanner, Pte W.W. 'Bob'	2,22,72		Wing, Pte A.	28
Taylor, Maj Nigel	xiv,42,52,167(p),168		Woodman, Lt/Capt/Maj E.E.	xv,89(p),104,105,156,161
Theobald, Lt Steve	xiv			
Thomas, Lt T.	xv,39,44,45,46,51,68,99,100		Woolcott, Pte G.	60
Todd, Lt/Capt Richard A.P.	3(p),144,161		Young, Capt A. (MO)	xiv,20,36(p)
Trafford, Pte R.H.	84,182		Young, Sgt S.	40,41
Troutt, Pte (RAMC)	139			
Trueman, Pte E.	118(p)			
Tullis, Maj R.	xiv,36			
Vian, Mme	47			
Villis, Sgt F.R.	167,182			
Vinci, Leonardo de	1			

7 Para Memorial
6th June 1944 - 4th September 1944

* Killed whilst training for D-Day

No.	Rank	Surname,	1st Name,	Initials	Died	Location and Memorial	
228433	Lt	Atkinson	Robert	N	7/7/44	Ranville	3A-L-1
5679154	Sgt	Balding	Leonard	G	9/6/44	Ranville	1A-A-22
14219568	Pte	Baldwin	John		19/8/44	Ranville	2A-D-14
5439144	Cpl	Ball	Frederick	W	22/8/44	Ranville	3A-C-5
14543706	Pte	Barratt	Peter		6/6/44	Ranville	3A-C-9
5678355	L/Cpl	Beard	Alfred	HJ	6/6/44	La Déliverande	4-K-4
5674103	Sgt	Beech	Joseph	A	6/6/44	La Déliverande	3-K-5
3254243	Pte	Bennett	Ralph	D	25/6/44	Ranville	4A-C-21
5679289	L/Cpl	Blackshaw	Eric	E	20/6/44	Ranville	4A-F-21
5387371	Sgt	Blakeway	Alexander	VS	23/8/44	Ranville	3A-F-5
151578	Lt	Bowler	John	A	7/6/44	Bayeux	Panel 18, col 1
176175	Capt	Bowyer	William		6/6/44	Bénouville Chyd	20
5679120	Pte ACC	Branson	William		10/6/44	Ranville	3A-B-5
14219916	Pte	Brookman	Herbert	ER	6/6/44	Ranville	1A-B-18
2184150	Pte	Burden	Alfred	L	10/8/44	Bayeux	Panel 18, col 1
2056538	Pte	Burgess	Kenneth	IH	6/6/44	Bénouville Chyd	14
6020537	Cpl	Bushell	Harold	R	26/8/44	Pont Audemer Comm Cem	28
3962078	Pte	Cavey	John		6/6/44	La Déliverande	4-K-6
5679083	L/Sgt	Chappel	Albert	E	6/6/44	Ranville	3A-G-8
14203394	Pte	Cooling	Harold	O	21/6/44	Le Déliverande	1-D-3
14405006	Pte	Copson	Geoffrey		6/6/44	Ranville	V1-AC-1/25
6923991	L/Cpl	Coulthard	Arthur	J	10/7/44	Ranville	4A-H-21
3976466	Pte	Davies	Elwyn	C	16/6/44	Ranville	1A-K-18
5679243	Cpl	Denham	Henry		6/6/44	La Déliverande	3-K-8
4693498	Pte KSLI	Downes	William	E	22/8/44	Ranville	3A-B-5
5674491	WO11	Durbin	Frederick	E	18/6/44	Bayeaux	Panel 18 col 1
5383220	Pte	Elmer	Alfred		6/6/44	Bénouville Chyd	3
14416229	Pte	Ely	Peter	OW	10/8/44	Bayeux	Panel 18 col 1
4039307	Pte KSLI	Evans	Sidney	H	26/8/44	Pont Audemer	Row A Grave 27
5675267	Sgt	Fay	Victor	C	19/8/44	Ranville	2A-M-9
1475163	Sgt	Fiddler	John	E	6/6/44	Bénouville Chyd	15
4032616	Pte	Finch	Peter	S	6/6/44	La Déliverande	4-K-5
14540720	Pte	Findley	James	M	18/6/44	Bayeaux	Panel 18 col 1
14000182	L/Cpl	Fisher	Charles	W	6/6/44	Bénouville Chyd	G-11
6921412	L/Cpl	Fox	Kenneth	F A	26/8/44	Dagenham Chyd	Not known
6354955	Pte	Francis	Reginald	AE	6/6/44	Ranville	4-A-C-1/25
14420431	Pte	Frost	Vincent	PC	6/6/44	Ranville	4-A-C-1/25
4546638	Pte	Garnett	Frederick		6/6/44	La Déliverande	3-K-7
4343281	L/Cpl	Gascoigne	John		6/6/44	Ranville	4-A-1-35
14219260	Pte	Gemmell	William		6/6/44	Bénouville Chyd	G-19
7620991	Pte RAOC	Grantham	Arthur	R	10/6/44	Ranville	1A-F-21
14436656	Pte	Gwilliam	Sydney	E	25/6/44	Ranville	3A-K-9

No.	Rank	Surname, 1st Name, Initials			Died	Location and Memorial	
3248506	Pte	Hand	George		18/6/44	Bayeaux	Panel 18 col 1
3782516	Cpl	Harding	James	P	6/6/44	Bayeux	10-A-4
5675290	L/Cpl	Hayward	Stanley	D	6/6/44	Bénouville Chyd	G1
14210029	Pte	Hek	William		6/6/44	La Délivrande	4-K-9
278546	Lt	Hill	Malcolm	R	6/6/44	Ranville	3-A-N-7
4035982	L/Cpl KSLI	Hindley	Edward		25/7/44	Hermanville	2-G-4
4042722	Pte KSLI	Hodges	George	F	7/7/44	Ranville	3A-K-1
14409029	Pte	Holdroyd	George	W	26/8/44	Ranville	VA-N-6
14364155	Pte	Hopgood	William	GA	6/6/44	Ranville Chyd	17
5679931	Sgt	Hounslow	Earnest	S	6/6/44	La Délivrande	4-K-11
14403536	Pte	Hughes	Patrick		6/6/44	La Délivrande	3-K-10
5674214	Pte	Huish	William	L	6/6/44	Herouvillette NCC	17
4470319	Cftmn REME	Hunt	George	W	6/6/44	Ranville	6A-C-1/25
5764216	WO11	Hutchings	John	EP	6/6/44	Ranville	6A-C-1/25
3253029	L/Cpl	Jackson	Frederick		6/6/44	Bénouville Chyd	25
5250009	Sgt	Jarvis	Ernest	W	6/6/44	La Délivrande	4-K-3
3191026	Pte	Johnston	James	B	10/6/44	Renville	1A-G-18
5250307	Pte	Jones	Ben		17/6/44	Maes-Y-Rar: An Cem Mountain 8369	
14641426	Pte	Kearns	James	P	6/6/44	Ranville	2A-0-2
14537124	Cpl	Kelly	Alfred	P	6/6/44	Ranville	2A-B-8
5676360	Cpl	Kemp	Alfred	R	6/6/44	Ranville	6A-C-1/25
5436300	Sgt	Kempster	Frank	G	19/8/44	Ranville	2A-D-13
3387613	Pte	Kerr	Dennis		6/6/44	La Délivrande	4-K-2
14514592	Pte KSLI	King	Michael	H	26/8/44	Pont Audemer Comm Cem	29
6856578	Pte	Kingsley	Robert		6/6/44	La Délivrande	3-K-9
14607558	Pte	Leadbetter	Robert		16/6/44	Hérouvillette Chyd	10A
5675357	Cpl	Leamer	George	H	6/6/44	Ranville	6A-C-1/25
5682680	Pte	Leary	Thomas	C	6/6/44	Ranville Chyd	46
5671819	Pte	Leslie	Wey	C	6/6/44	La Délivrande	4-K-joint grave 11
97003530	Pte RAMC	Lidell	Donald	S	21/6/44	La Délivrande	1-D-3
1400090	Pte	Lothian	Alex		6/6/44	Ranville	1A-C-8
278379	Lt	Macdonald	Ian	G	29/6/44	Ranville	3A-B-9
3251685	Pte	McAra	John		6/6/44	Bénouville Chyd	5
14418286	Pte	McCann	Terence	K	10/6/44	La Délivrande	5A-F-3
3251502	Cpl	McCulloch	James	A	19/6/44	La Délivrande	1-D-1
14216814	Pte	McGee, DCM	Michael	J	6/6/44	Bénouville Chyd	12
5671017	Pte	Metcalfe	Charles	E	10/6/44	Ranville	5A-F-4
14408742	Pte	Mills	Raymond	H	6/6/44	Bénouville Chyd	16
3066484	L/Cpl	Mitchell	Robert	L	6/6/44	Ranville	6A-C-1/25
1139320	Pte	Mortimer	John	H	6/6/44	Ranville	3A-N-8
295223	Pte	Mundy	Ernest	H	13/6/44	Walthamstow Chyd Grave 2749	
14412168	Pte	O'Brian	James	R	23/8/44	Ranville	VA-Q-1
14381097	Pte	Padley	Albert		6/6/44	Ranville	3A-M-8
3252435	Cpl	Panton	Douglas	D	6/6/44	Bénouville Chyd	7
173033	Revd RACHD	Parry	George	EM	6/6/44	Ranville Chyd	21
14406064	L/Cpl	Pegg	William	F	20/6/44	Ranville	4A-E-21

The Tale of Two Bridges

No.	Rank	Surname, 1st Name, Initials		Died	Location and Memorial	
5680060	L/Cpl	Phillips	Leslie H	6/6/44	La Déliverande	4-K-7
14404617*	Pte	Prendergrass	Christopher T	4/1/44	Ilford, Barkingside	
5340704	L/Cpl	Price	Sydney A	10/7/44	Ranville	4A-K-21
5393694	Pte	Rawlings	Edward JC	20/6/44	Hermanville	1-W-19
5678261	Pte	Reed	Clifford W	10/6/44	Ranville	1A-E-21
14410593	Pte	Reid	Gordon	7/7/44	Ranville	3A-E-3
14327631	Pte	Rennie	John R	6/6/44	Ranville	9-C-34
3769861	Pte	Riley	Leonard	6/6/44	Ranville	1-E110
14203815	Pte	Roast	Albert E	23/6/44	Hermanville	3-B-6
5339074	Pte	Roberts	George S	11/6/44	Ranville	5A-C-2
5679569*		Russell	Harold WJ	31/12/43	Bristol Cmty	
5054148	Pte	Saunders	Alfred	6/6/44	Ranville	3A-O-8
3244621	CQMS	Savill	Stanley C	14/6/44	Ranville	2A-N-10
14663800	Pte	Schwartz	Donald R	6/6/44	Bayeux	Panel 18 col 1
3251811	Pte	Scott	Walter	6/6/44	Ranville	6A-C-1/25
5679544	Cpl	Sheldon	Charles H	10/6/44	Bayeux	Panel 18 col 1
14218485	Pte	Shutt	Dennis	6/6/44	Ranville	6A-C-1/25
5434512	Pte	Smith	Frederick	6/6/44	Ranville	5A-G-2
4469397	Pte	Smith	John W	6/6/44	La Déliverande SP	C3-K-6
5678125*	Sgt	Stenner	Edward A	26/3/44	Bristol Cmty	
2026577	Pte	Stobart	Robert W	6/6/44	Ranville	6-A-C-1/25
14407652	Pte	Stringer	Charles K	6/6/44	La Déliverande	4-K-1
14578482	Pte	Stubbins	Cyril C	6/6/44	La Déliverande	3-K-17
5498650	Pte	Surman	Cyril J	6/6/44	La Déliverande	4-K-8
5835746	Pte	Sutton	Christopher F	6/6/44	Ranville	3A-O-7
14000069	Pte	Swan	John FM	18/644	Ranville	4A-L-21
14401886	Pte	Taplin	Henry F	7/6/44	Ranville	4-A-K12
130115	Capt	Temple	William AB	16/644	Dagenham	Grave 663
14430681	Pte	Thompson	Samual C	6/6/44	Bayeux	Panel 18 col 2
14417638	L/Cpl	Thompson	Barry B	22/8/44	Ranville	3A-D-5
14275596	Pte	Trafford	Ronald H	7/7/44	Ranville	3A-M-1
1420750	Pte	Trotman	harold C	18/6/44	Ranville	4A-P-21
14209955	Pte	Trueman	Montague J	6/6/44	La Déliverande	4-K-10
3244791	L/Cpl	Twist	Robert	6/6/44	Ranville	6A-C-1/25
5676770	Cpl	Van-Rynen	Albert	6/6/44	Ranville	6A-C-1/25
5392732	Pte	Varney	Alfred T	10/7/44	La Déliverande	3-H-9
5670432	Sgt	Villis	Francis R	7/6/44	Hermanville	1-B-3
4469400	Pte	Vincent	Kenneth	7/6/44	Hermanville	1-B-12
4865382	Pte	Walker	John	6/6/44	La Déliverande	3-K-8
14421370	Pte	Webster	John D	10/8/44	Ranville	6A-B-18
5671819	Pte	Wey	L C	6/6/44	La Déliverande	4-K-11
14301841	L/Cpl	Whittingham	Peter A	6/6/44	Bénouville Chyd	G-17
888352	Pte	Whitty	Allan W	6/6/44	Bénouville Chyd	G-10
6925114	Pte	Williams	Daniel R	10/7/44	Ranville	4A-G-21
6852353	Cpl	Wilson	William C	20/8/44	Ranville	2A-J-4
14000138	Pte	Woodgate	Dennis A	20/6/44	Ranville	3A-N-1

> 7TH LIGHT INFANTRY BATTALION
> THE PARACHUTE REGIMENT
>
> IN MEMORY OF THOSE WHO DIED
> HOLDING THIS BRIDGEHEAD
> 6 JUNE 1944
> A LA MÉMOIRE DE CEUX QUI ONT TROUVÉ
> LA MORT EN DEFENDANT CETTE TÊTE DE PONT

"They shall not grow old as we who are left grow old,
Age shall not weary them, nor the years condemn,
At the going down of the sun, and in the morning
we shall remember them."

(Laurence Binyon 1864-1945)

In this the new millennium it is a forgotten fact, due to the mists of time, that by 0240hrs on June 6th 1944 the 7th Battalion was in position in Bénouville, with the coup-de-main party in reserve between the bridges. Both Battalions had achieved their objectives, to capture and hold, at all costs, both of the bridges. Both Companies held forward flank with honour.

Prayer of Airborne Forces

May the defence of the Most High be above and beneath,
around and within us, in our going out and our coming in,
in our rising up and our going down,
through all our days and all our nights,
until dawn when the Sun of Righteousness shall rise
with healing in his wings for the peoples of the world,
through Jesus Christ Our Lord.

Amen.